WRITING
self
and the moral

WRITING

self

and the moral

Berel •
Lang •

Routledge · New York & London

Published in 1991 by

Routledge
An imprint of Routledge, Chapman and Hall, Inc.
29 West 35 Street
New York, NY 10001

Published in Great Britain by

Routledge
11 New Fetter Lane
London EC4P 4EE

Library of Congress Cataloging in Publication Data

Lang, Berel.
    Writing and the moral self / Berel Lang.
      p. cm.
    Includes bibliographical references and index.
    ISBN 0-415-90295-9. — ISBN 0-415-90296-7 (pbk.)
    1. Language and ethics. 2. English language—Philosophy.
3. Style (Philosophy) I. Title.
BJ44.L36 1991
808'.001—dc20   90-25234

British Library Cataloguing in Publication Data

Lang, Berel.
    Writing and the moral self.
    1. Rhetoric
    I. Title.
    808
    ISBN 0-415-90295-9
    ISBN 0-415-90296-7 pbk

Forrest, Joel, Tuvia
for whom words live

Table of Contents

vii

II: Rewriting in the Academy

III: Politics at More Than Its Word

CONTENTS

Introduction

The essays in this volume were written during more than a decade and on a variety of occasions—or, as they often seemed to me, provocations. Most have been published previously, although in periodicals or anthologies so diverse in their themes (and sometimes so far out of the way) that few readers would be likely to have encountered many of the pieces, or to have considered the connection among them if they did. This is not by itself, I realize, a justification for gathering them here, and they will in any event have to make their own ways now as before. But in bringing the essays together, I first discovered and now find myself hoping to confirm in them two common themes—one that defines a literary framework which accounts for their form and "manner" (directed also, then, to readers' expectations); the second, a substantive feature which, in the way of genealogy, indicates their common origin or, less delicately, their cause.

The first of these involves the combination of a manner of discourse with a genre of writing. The manner—I suppose I should claim only an *intended* manner—aims for a middle ground between the technical abstraction of "learned" discourse designed to win a permanent foothold on a frictionless surface, and the consumable writing of journalism, meant to glow and to disappear almost simultaneously. I have written and read in both these forms widely enough to recognize that to do either of them well demands commitment and skill; certainly each serves genuine needs or at least "wants." My objection, then, is not to those forms of writing individually but to their constant rejection of each other—a mutual antagonism which they seem willing to put aside only when they establish a common front against *other* alternatives. The two forms, in other words, demand that writers (and readers) choose not only between them, but *exclusively* between them, as though together they spanned the world of writing.

1

This insistence seems to me at once to exaggerate and to diminish the claims that the two forms of writing are entitled to make, individually or together. There is no incompatibility between the hope for mastery in the first of them and the swiftness and immediacy of the other; there should then be a third way that, as it highlights the contrasting features of the others, also contributes to a fuller, more "realistic" map of the topography of writing. The genre most likely to serve as a means for this alternative has seemed—seems—obvious. The essay, which in its literal origins aspires only to the role of an "attempt," essays first the self of a writer; aware of the many temptations to reach beyond itself, the genre cannot hope to escape the conditions that, together with the author's self, hold it back. These conditions, although familiar, are not often enough stated, probably because to those for whom they are not obviously false, they seem too obviously true: on the one hand, that even the hardest facts cannot be too hard to be human; on the other hand, that even for the freest, most independent self, history is inescapable. These are portentous truths to attach to works as slight in their dimensions as many of the essays collected here. But it is the genre—what they might have been—that such claims disclose; literary form is itself, after all, also an idea.

The substantive theme that links the essays similarly challenges a bifurcated or dualistic world. My intention here has in part been to join the now common refrain against the traditional distinction between form and content, affirming instead the connection between them—at the mid-point, as it must then be, between the form of the content and the content of the form. Even beyond that, however, I have hoped to give writing and language themselves the last word. The imagination, reacting against the partisan networks of history, understandably dreams of a neutral instrument—a medium at once transparent and subservient that would not speak for itself but would do only as it was told. Among human artifacts, writing has not been the only competitor for this role, but it has been the strongest and most persistent one, more so even than thought—since, unlike thinking, writing has also the *appearance* of intractibility. Like stones or hills, marks and signs do not have to worry about what they are, where they come from, where they are going; they seem small enough and pliable enough to do all and only what they are told, to hold nothing back. Here there should be no servant problem.

2

And yet: the concept of an ideal language that serves without expectation or regret, that admits neither the uncertainty of an open future nor the constraints of a historical past—in other words, that would escape the human subject—has proved illusory, the more painfully so because the prospect is so tempting. Like the philosopher's stone, it would produce gold; like the philosopher's stone, it shows only that matter—including now language and writing—is recalcitrant. The fact that writing is firmly attached to history means, even if we knew nothing else about it, that it does not exist without friction, without being affected by the world outside it and to this extent disclosing the form of that world as well. What writing is "about" has much the same character; here, too, there is no way of telling the dancer from the dance. The what and the how of writing thus converge, adding that convergence to the text itself.

What happens when we do acknowledge a connection between the means and ends of writing, when the two meet in a particular appearance? The next questions tumble out, elbowing each other for place, the high-minded jostling the venial: What good or harm does the act accomplish? Who is responsible? Who benefits? Is there intention? Or should we speak rather of cause? What constitutes virtue (if it is not only the "just" word)? And sin (original or not)? There emerges, in short, as for any other declaration of agency, ethics—the measure of what should be against the reality of what is. Observed from this perspective, the writer's self is always in motion, advancing on the "other" (that is, the reader), affecting that other for good or ill, rightly or wrongly. Writing about writing, if it does not begin with this concern, must sooner or later come to it.

The essays in the present volume did not set out individually to "do" ethics; they make no claim together of providing a system. But as a group they point in a number of the directions that writing, as an act of and about ethics, may take—structurally in displaying its means, intentionally as the writing realizes (or fails to realize) ends that involve much more than words. The essays may fall short of their own standards in these "attempts"—but even where this occurs, it is not, I should claim, because they muddy waters that are otherwise clear. Obviously, the essays are unlikely to discover in writing everything to be found there, or to say about what they see all that needs to be said. They would fail far beyond this, though, if it were not evident in them that what they find in the *fact* of the connection between writing and ethics, they have not put there themselves.

The essays in Part I, "The Ethics of Language," address the individual terms of that relation: for ethics, referring to the treatment of certain persons or groups, and for language, marking the early point where it discloses the intention (and thus the responsibility) of its writers or speakers. Strunk and White's *Elements of Style* is not by conventional standards a study of ethics. But it seems to me impossible to read that book or to explain its continued appeal without recognizing a representation of moral character in its description of the conventions of grammar and style— including all the possibilities for good, evil, and mischance that moral character is subject to in its more deliberately literary or philosophical appearances. The book's modesty in refusing to make that claim is itself part of this representation; the style it recommends and the terms it uses, with their challenge to dishonesty or pretense in writing—to the avoidance of responsibility—would, without admitting this connection, be simply arbitrary, surely the last word one would apply to that text.

This theme in the opening essay, "Strunk, White, and Grammar as Morality," also shapes the other essays in the first section—arguing the "rights of Black English" and the relation between "pronouns and affirmative action"; disputing the tendentious concept of "pre-literacy" at the same time that it anticipates the odd phenomenon of "post-literacy"; pointing to linguistic change in the term *truth* as a clue to a shift in moral reflection—and to misconceptions of the relation between writer and reader that have skewed the definitions of pornography and obscenity. The ethics of language that finds its first objects in grammar and syntax thus shows their connection—in effect, their grounds—in larger and more familiar issues of moral judgment.

The essays in Part II, "Rewriting in the Academy," focus on the recent history of writing in the university—an institution where, more decisively than for any other, writing has been at once a means and a subject. The methods and goals of science have dominated the "higher learning" in its rapid post–World War II evolution; one consequence of this has been a growing distance between claims for objectivity and "disinterested" knowledge, on the one hand, and the stubborn, untidy, and unavoidably personal reference of ethical questions, on the other. Predictably, the same split between facts and values has surfaced in academic writing, giving a public face to the institution. Ideology tends here as elsewhere to conceal itself, but rarely has its presence been more evident than in the authority asserted by scientific discourse—over writing (and thinking) in the "humane" no less than in the "natural" sciences.

It becomes increasingly important, then, to trace the appearances of this assertion of authority, especially since the ideal turns so quickly back on itself: objectivity, disinterestedness, the stance of impersonality are no less (and no less obviously) values than their opposites. It is too much to assert that in their consequences for writing, such features are only stylistic; but clearly they are *also* stylistic—the thesis developed in the first essay of this section, "Academics and the English Language." The implications of this "tendency" for teaching and learning (and for the university as an institution) are extensive. On the one hand, they converge in the one value openly endorsed in that "value-free" setting, namely, the tolerance for differences—in opinions, theories, and then, by implication, among persons and groups. Admittedly, the word of this endorsement has been more fulsome than the act. But the word has nonetheless had its effect, and undoubtedly more broadly than its first proponents had conceived or would have wished. The grade to be assigned here, I suggest, like so many others, is not for brilliance or failure, but for "normal academic progress."

On the other hand, tolerance itself, privileged over other values and held apart from them, comes at a price. Conceptually, it contributes to a failure of nerve even at the point where the need for distinctions is least deniable; left to itself, the principle of tolerance would not yield even the idea of limits. For some issues addressed in the university, this consequence ends with a dilemma from which there seems to be no escape—a fact that I and many others have discovered in efforts at "teaching the Holocaust." In another, psychological implication, the result has been a withdrawal and narrowing—the professionalized hope for a type of security made possible only by sacrificing the imagination and its uncertain future. In these terms, the "New Scholasticism" is not a phantom, but a demand of the academy itself—the culmination of a process that someone in the university is undoubtedly "researching" at this moment (no doubt under the title "The History of the Footnote").

It has been fashionable recently to base suspicion of writing in the present on an invidious comparison to the past. This hopeful nostalgia, in my view, only adds historical misrepresentation to a misunderstanding of the present—not only because there is in any event no going back to the past, but because the cure prescribed would not work even if it could be applied. It is more than only an irony that many of those who decry present learning in favor of its counterpart in the past would have no place from which to do this were it not for changes in the university that are inseparable from what they now object to there. The ideal of universal education is undoubtedly the single most important principle that the academy in the United States has fostered, one that is still unique to it. That this ideal has exacted a toll in learning and writing is not irrelevant, but neither is it a warrant for the sentimentality, let alone for the proposals of repression, that have often appeared in responses to it. This objection to a common misrepresentation of writing and learning in the university is the theme of the two essay-reviews of books in which the shadow of nostalgia dominates: "The Humanities in American Life" and "About the Dead, Speak _____Only _____Mainly _____Some _____No Good."

Classical social theory, as in Plato and Aristotle, argued that politics was "prior" to ethics; and recent history has supported the application of this claim to the politics of writing and language. Although the act of writing or speaking recalls most immediately an individual hand or voice, the awareness has become increasingly compelling that even those individual acts occur in a social context that expresses itself both through and around the writer. George Orwell was not the first or only observer of totalitarianism to recognize that control over language, spoken and written, was intrinsic to its design. But few writers have combined his grasp of the practical devices of totalitarianism with an imagination that could predict what those devices would amount to as lived; still fewer have succeeded in contrasting the nightmare of this world with the requirements—no less dependent on the imagination, it has to be said—of non- or anti-totalitarian writing. The first two essays of Part III—"Politics at

6

More Than Its Word''—consider this contrast first in the terms that Orwell himself specifies, and then as those terms shape his own writing. Indifferent, even hostile to theory, Orwell saw as a practical matter that writing could not point to anything else without first pointing to itself. This is, it seems to me, an implication of democratic politics for the structure of writing—a gesture that one of the essays on Orwell notices also in the writing of Thoreau and that is argued again in an essay on Thoreau, ''The Body Impolitic.''

The last essays of Part III, ''Hannah Arendt and the Politics of Evil'' and ''Language and Genocide,'' identify a role for language and writing in the specific historical occurrence of the Nazi genocide against the Jews. It might seem that in confronting this event, language or even politics is the least of the matter; the most evident victims there were not words or laws but people. Yet as soon as the question is addressed of how the process of that genocide unfolded, how it was *possible,* the marks left by and on language appear not only as symptom but as cause. It is one thing to predict, as Orwell did, the syntax of an ''ideal'' totalitarian language; it is another thing to see an actual language, nourished by centuries of cultural intensity, take on the same features that distinguish the act of genocide. Like all expression, the language of genocide in part discloses its character involuntarily; totalitarian language much prefers to conceal and obscure. But intention is evident here even so—further proof, given the attempted concealment, that language and writing are also products of will and consciousness, that is, of a responsible agent. An implication of the relation between ''writing and the moral self,'' then, is that the same relation holds between language and evil, that is, between writing and the *im*moral self. So at least, in both evidence and principle, history seems to attest.

Writers who take writing itself as their subject know that they will be read, or at least watched, more closely than if they were writing about other subjects. They would be naive if they failed to anticipate that the standards they direct at other writing will quickly be applied to their own. Such reflexive criticism, it seems to me, is not only understandable but just; readers have almost no other recourse when faced by a writer's moralizing. But this same scrutiny, like other categorical tests, also virtually ensures a verdict of failure, at moments if not constantly; even the knowledge of that fate beforehand can do little to hinder it.

I hope it will be clear, then, that these essays come with no claims of impunity. Nor do I doubt the applicability to them of certain general principles that might seem to qualify or at least to anticipate the particular claims they make; for example, the valuable lesson taught by recent theorists that writing, whatever its overt subject, is also always "about" writing. Undoubtedly, there is a measure of Schadenfreude in the discovery that tough-minded pragmatists who admit as "real" only things and consequences are forced to concede that tender-minded theory has a hold even on that claim—but this does not weaken the discovery either in general or as it applies in particular to the act and consequences of writing. The Marxist tradition of criticism offers no less pointed a lesson about the social conscience of writing, with its disclosure of the way that silence and repression—the gaps in or around writing—are themselves part of any text.

All these subtleties would be pointless, however, without an awareness of the most basic, or at least the most flagrant truth for all writing: that in it someone (the writer) *does* something to someone else (the reader). The form of responsibility in this applies not only to writing but to all morally relevant acts; the question it evokes in respect to the essays collected here, then, is not *whether* a relation exists between writing and ethics, but only *how* the relation expresses itself and what means it employs (or avoids). Thus, as the connection between writing and ethics is emblematic of the writer's art as a whole, the same relation constantly challenges the reader's understanding and judgment. And with this as a basis, it is no surprise that writing about writing would then find a central theme in the relation between writing and ethics.

I The Ethics of Language

1

Strunk, White, and Grammar as Morality

The complaints are endless about the current state of writing and reading. Teachers are not teaching, and students are not learning, and if that symmetry continues—the students with age turning into teachers—we can easily predict the outcome. Is it possible that literacy was only a response to a one-time need and appears now in its later, natural decline? We could, after all, argue this case too from symmetry. The post-literate culture that stores its learning in computers would then complete a circle that had started with the oral epic and folktale of pre-literate societies; at either of those two moments, writing and reading were, would be, beside the point. But we cannot be certain that history is bound to repeat itself in this way, and so we continue to quarrel with the new illiteracy.

Admittedly, nostalgia is one of the few sentiments that technology encourages (a way of verifying that the past is gone before quite burying it), and reminiscing about the age of literacy often has just this aura of summoning a past that will never return. On a second side, we meet also the practical argument from technology itself—that writing even now remains necessary for transmitting information, that computer programs too start out from ordinary language and are limited by the precision and clarity which that language commands. But these finally seem to be only small parts of the issue, since the complaints about writing have been less practical than moral in tone—moral in their judgment and moral in their condemnation. Bad writing, we are to understand, is bad not only as writing but because bad writing is itself bad, a form of wrongdoing, related to other and more lurid ethical faults. Corporate and white-collar crime, lying in government, possibly the overt acts of social violence as well: these almost always involve deception, evasion, the will to get something for nothing, and they are usually committed by people who

pretend to be what they are not and who do not know how to become it—
precisely the conditions under which bad writing flourishes.

Is bad writing *criminal?* we may then ask skeptically. There is evidently
no court of law in which to try such offenses, but the moral testimony is
hard to ignore. On any except the crudest and most mechanical view,
writing is expressive even when it is attempting to be only informative;
often we can hardly distinguish between what is expressed and what is
asserted, between style and substance, form and content. That connection
is probably more obvious in non-literary arts (in music, for example, or
painting), but poetry and fiction provide ready examples as well, and even
non-fictional discourse sharply reveals the face of its author to any reader
who takes the writer at something more than his word. It does not require
McLuhan, let alone Freud or Marx, to point out that the *way* something
is said or written will itself be part of *what* is being said or written: how
could writing *not* carry the mark of its origins? We speak of "Dickens"
or "Jane Austen" when we mean to refer to what those writers wrote,
and this is more than just a use of shorthand: close to their books, so
close as to leave little space between book and reader, is the person and
voice which shape the writing. A reader would no more confuse works
by these two authors than he would mistake one of his good friends for
another—and the relation between those forms of identification is more
than metaphorical.

As expression reveals the agent, the relation of them both to the character of that agent soon appears as well. Actions both constitute the person
and reveal him; we cannot imagine character so hidden or deep that it
will not show itself in action. It is worth noting in this connection that the
term *character* itself is part of the history of writing, originally referring
in Greek to a tool for marking or engraving and then subsequently to the
"characters" of writing—the letters that *were engraved;* then moving to
the hand, the person, and finally to the 'character' of the writer. (Almost
the same history recurs for the Latin *stylus;* it, too, is first an instrument,
for inscribing on a wax tablet, which then detaches itself to become the
writer's own "style.")

These echoes are at least circumstantial evidence for a connection between writing and morality, and criticism about the decline of writing is
often quite precise in the diagnosis of moral failing. It hardly goes much

12

beyond the evidence to infer from a paragraph in which tenses or objects are confused that the confusion was first in the thinking of the writer; or that if careless argument is offered to a reader as cogent, both—the carelessness and the offer—are the responsibility of the writer. We make these inferences not because *all* actions reflect the hands or heads of their agents (if this is true, it is not especially so for writing), but because of an unusual immediacy in the connection between writing and character. It is there as if the hand *were* the head—an identity we accept more readily as we recognize that writing doesn't have much to do with hands at all. (Graphologists claim to identify the writer only by his handwriting; consider then the weight that the *content* of writing adds to this identification.)

Does the connection between writing and the writer mean that the unending casuistry and legalism of handbooks on writing with their often shrill insistence on obedience to grammar are actually only versions of ethical instruction? That corrections of punctuation or spelling are simply disguises for moral education? The cunning of history has produced stories no less fanciful than this, and once we recognize the intentional design of grammars and styles, the discovery that those intentions are expressive is no more startling than finding that other human gestures are; the surprise, in fact, would be the other way. To be sure, if writing were only a technique or skill—like driving a car or hammering a nail—then our interest in it would be only instrumental, restricted to the question of what we can do with it. But one clue in the structure of writing itself that should make us wary of this view is the fact that the only system of rules in literate societies as complex and emphatically prescriptive as the control over writing is the moral code, the regulations decreeing what is permissible or forbidden in conduct. The structural analogy between these systems does not prove a substantive connection between them, but it reinforces what their common tone suggests more immediately. The anthropologist's idiom of totem and taboo, the religious distinction between the sacred and profane, the sociological confession of norms and legitimation—these all are variations on a theme that extends the lines of demarcation in an ethos and social order to the grammatical and stylistic conventions of writing. Hayden White, expanding on Jonathan Swift's definition of style ("Proper words in proper places"), applies to the structure of writing the ingenious conceit of "Style and Incest"—warning that writers, too, must not put the wrong things in the wrong places. We could stop well short of this absorption of grammar into cultural taboo and still find room for the social status of grammatical rules—partly in their function as rules, partly as they provide a syntax for conduct.

The oldest, most persistent theory of literary discourse conceives of that discourse as representational, directing the reader to a reference beyond the discourse itself. On this account, the *rules* of writing must also be representational: the purpose they serve would have to appear first in the directions for realizing it. We find this intuition borne out, in fact, in the current wonder of the publishing world: the proliferation of "How-to-Do-It" books—how to fix a car, how to fix a marriage, how to find God—of which handbooks of style and writing are one group. From the variety and number of such texts alone, it seems likely that often their readers are content to substitute the reading of their instruction for actually carrying them out. Even for readers who do more than this (and certainly for those who do not), however, there is the pleasure of the representations themselves, the comfort in them of fictional and idealized worlds, of regularity, control. This attraction is still more intense when the idealized world is that of language and writing. There, too, the reader is drawn by a glimpse of imagined power and vicarious strength, as the space in his experience taken up by language is brought more fully under his control. Once learn the "how" of writing—a bargain is struck with the reader—and the "what" will take care of itself. The one important human activity for which the connection between these two is otherwise first promised and then realized in practice is in moral conduct.

I have been arguing for grammar as morality in general terms when writing, the handbooks insist, should be concrete, specific. It was in fact a notable one of these guides—Strunk and White's *Element of Style*—that started these reflections on the moral standing of the rules of writing, and certainly, in *that* book, the connection is openly made and systematically observed. This is not to say that *Elements of Style* is systematic in its own exposition. For one thing, it is too brief to serve as a system of rhetoric (eighty-five short pages), and Strunk and White also treat quite casually the order in which questions of style and grammar (the two are constantly mixed together) are taken up. Who would guess, for example, that the first question in a text designed to improve writing would ask whether the possessive form of "Charles" should add an apostrophe and an *s* or only an apostrophe? (Strunk and White conclude that it should be "Charles's.") Strunk and White are also short on history (they're proposing changes in *future* conduct, after all), and they are not much inclined to justify the commands they freely give. "Do," "Don't," "Use," "Avoid," "Omit," "Keep,"—the reader is constantly ordered about, and if the orders do not persuade by their own force, they will not persuade at all. The reader who insists on reasons or who tends to resist authority will quickly find the surroundings inhospitable.

But the book's popularity is hardly due to either its literary brevity or its shortness of temper, or even to its modest and homespun manner. (So, for example, Strunk and White consider the word *prestigious:* "Often an adjective of last resort. It's in the dictionary, but that doesn't mean you have to use it.") More basic than these qualities, although surely related to them, is the comfort to be found in the book, a warmth that readers may associate more often with the mixture of concern and honesty that only good friends—and people who are good at being friends—provide. In books, this presents itself with the recognition by the writer of a common humanity with his reader—a commonality in both ideals and mortality. For the small price of a book, then, Strunk and White offer a gift of fellowship and counsel. There is nothing soft or tender-minded in this generosity; they speak sharply, often harshly, always without compromise. But the limits they set for their readers never aggrandize the authors at their readers' expense. The work to be done, and so the chances and consequences of success, are shared, if only because success will benefit all readers and writers. The good sought, moreover, is not the good of simple utility, however one might first suspect the practical intentions of grammar or punctuation. (Writing, Levi-Strauss argues, first came into existence as another weapon of the ruling class; but even if this were so, that device, like others traced to the same origin, has clearly gotten out of hand.) Strunk and White know the importance of writing as a means of conveying information, but the clarity and precision—the *simplicity*—that in their view best serve communication are not primarily the means to another end: like other moral qualities, the values of good writing are, first, good in themselves.

Allegory is not now written or considered as a popular genre of writing—but this judgment itself may be misleading since we know that readers find themselves most effectively in the presence of allegory (as with myth) when they are least conscious of the fact. The Greek myths were not "myths" for the Greeks, and what now appears as discursive and abstract in Bunyan's *Pilgrim's Progress*—characters named after virtues or vices that we might not now even acknowledge—was almost certainly more fully integrated in the sensibility of its original audience. Dead allegories thus stand in relation to live allegories as dead or broken metaphors stand in relation to live ones (one difference is that the self-consciousness that gives life to metaphor is what kills allegory)—and *Elements of Style* comes close in fact to just such a representation of live allegory. In it, we see the outline of a continuing struggle between moral forces—a struggle carried on by Strunk and White for the side of the good under the guise of grammatical instruction, in a Manichean world where pretention, pomposity, tactlessness, and opacity pit their easy charms against simplicity, directness, sincerity.

For Strunk and White, the terms of this opposition are characters in a drama, and there is thus no need to explain or to rationalize them. *Why* is it desirable to practice "moderation" (a "main consideration in paragraphing") and "simplicity" (the "use of colloquialisms without calling attention to them by quotation marks")? Well, because the alternatives are clearly wrong and bad—and if a reader requires proof of *that,* he is unlikely to understand any other part of the story either. Strunk and White, in the Yankee grain, are impatient and brief in both their writing and their temper. The moral comfort they offer comes mainly, in fact, as an invitation to independence, to autonomy. No one can do for the writer what he must do for himself; there is no place for him to hide, no means by which he can avoid revealing himself. Concealment, for the written word, is a form of deception, with deception the basic or capital crime, larger even than carelessness or ineptitude, although the three often collaborate.

Listen for a moment to what Strunk and White object to in the misuses and misusers of grammar or style: they are "showy" (for the purveyors of "thrust"—as in the "thrust of the discussion"—that "darling of executives, politicos, and speech-writers"); they are "pompous" (when they complete what they are doing by "finalizing" it), they are "fancy" (culti-

16

vating the "elaborate, the pretentious, the coy, and the cute"), "show-offs" (as they "sprinkle their works with foreign expressions").

Such temptations to sin have the quality often of lying and always of vainglory. The writer who exhibits himself at the expense of his object is dishonest at once to his reader and to his writing. It is not only that pretentiousness is to be avoided, moreover, since this leaves over the question of what qualities writing will disclose when it is *not* pretending to be something it is not, when it is not "ambiguous," "fuzzy," "vague," "noncommittal," "irresolute." Not only should writing not pretend to be other than it is, then, but it must be unequivocal in its own claims, without hedge or compromise. Writing should be "concise," "careful," and most of all, "definite"—and so, we infer, must be the objects of the writing itself. The importance of these qualities in writing thus has as much to do with life as with writing—even more, if we acknowledge with Strunk and White that the most that writing can hope to realize for itself are the qualities of what the writing is written about. "The approach to style is by way of plainness, simplicity, orderliness, sincerity. . . . Muddiness is not merely a disturber of prose, it is also a destroyer of life, of hope."

To summarize the ideals of written style for Strunk and White, then, is to compose a model of human character: honest, plain, forthright, patient, simple. These qualities, we imagine, would have been valued as moral virtues well before the invention—or should it be the discovery?—of writing, but in writing we see them (or their absence) wonderfully displayed. Admittedly, if we step back from the portrait drawn by Strunk and White, we recognize that theirs is not the only likely ideal for either writing or character. It is uncertain, for example, how the prose or persons of Gibbon or Henry James or Emerson would stand inspection by Strunk and White, and even the striking virtues of plainness or simplicity that might be claimed for the writing of Thoreau or Emily Dickinson or in Strunk and White themselves often turn out not to be simple or plain after all. But the fact that there are alternate ideals of writing or even concealed depths in this one does not fault the model that Strunk and White hold up, any more than the existence of many moral qualitities is an objection to the work of a few of them. Certainly it does not hinder their claim for the moral standing of the written work just in its appearance as written.

The belief is unconditional for Strunk and White that writing is not something added to the writer's character, but a part of it; it too attests to a common history, a common series of choices, and a common issue. As writers, we can do well or badly by one as by the other, but no one should doubt that it is indeed we who are doing this and that in writing we show as much of ourselves as we have to show—often more than we would otherwise choose to admit.

2

Pre-literacy, Post-literacy, and the Cunning of History

Literacy is usually taken to be a descriptive, not a normative concept, but the use of the term in everyday life tells another story. There, literacy, in addition to its neutral designation of the ability to read and to write (why, one might ask, should those be so automatically linked? We easily imagine readers who cannot write and perhaps even a society which had so extended its division of labor), has other and stronger connotations. Certainly *illiterate* is a pejorative term, often used as an insult—and even *non-literate* and *pre-literate* carry with them a sense of the primitive, the undeveloped. Far better, we understand, if the individuals or cultures to whom those terms apply were able to read and write. And no less striking than this implication is the connotation in the concept of literacy of its inevitability—the supposition that pre-literate societies or the pre-literate ages of societies are no more than precursors to literacy, thus also that culture, certainly "high" culture, *requires* the advance to literacy. Not to be literate is often taken to imply that one has nothing worth writing or reading *about*.

Two features in particular of the latter assumption are worth considering. The first of these is the way in which the assumption conflates history and necessity, invoking the history of certain cultures (mainly that of Western Europe) as a general model of history to which all cultural groups must or, more strongly, *will* conform. The second feature is the way in which literacy is seen as an endpoint or goal. Pre-literacy is conceived as preliminary to literacy—but literacy itself is not seen as even potentially transient: it is the terminus or stopping point to which pre-literate cultures reach and around which more advanced cultures circle. Since the greatest intellectual and social achievements that we recognize are associated with literate societies, it is not surprising that we should assume first a causal connection between these two variables and then the fixed and permanent role of literacy in *any* intellectual achievement—or that we should forget that these are indeed assumptions.

The effect of these presuppositions is to obscure the historical character of literacy—the fact that, as for all cultural phenomena, social and material causes propel the transition here from pre-literacy to literacy and that there is thus nothing natural or inevitable about the transition. Even more importantly, the fact is obscured that as historical and material factors have unmistakably influenced the origins of literacy, those same or analogous factors may also contribute to or even invite its *disappearance.* As we look for historical explanation, we cannot avoid taking into account the needs and interests of social groups which affect whatever is being explained; and if the origins of literacy are linked to such needs or interests, then the conclusion is unavoidable that should the latter disappear or should a more compelling institutional response to them become available, literacy might well lose its function and thus itself be likely to disappear.

The point here is that we ought to begin to think of literacy as a social institution, for it has all of the latter's characteristic features: it is the result of a corporate and cumulative effort; it provides a framework to which individual members of the (literate) group adapt themselves; it even has an administrative hierarchy and authority, visible in the grammarians and lexicographers; and, most of all, it serves a quite evident, if various, social function. Once we admit literacy as an institution, moreover, we will recognize also that, like any institution, it has both a contingent past— it exists now, although it might not have—and a contingent future: it may or may not continue to have a function.

At that point, too, it becomes difficult to ignore the specific causes responsible for this development of literacy into an institution. Any such retrospective history will, of course, be speculative—but that is less because the origins of literacy are obscured in the past than because the explanation of even *current* historical phenomena is unavoidably speculative. Let me mention two such prospective explanations of the phenomenon of literacy, each of them with some theoretical and historical sanction. (The two are not incompatible with each other.)

The first of these accounts describes literacy as an extension of memory, providing for the storage and accumulation of bits of information that would otherwise be inaccessible or simply lost. So Plato reports in the *Phaedrus* an older Egyptian myth:

> Theuth it was that invented number and calculation, geometry and astrono-my . . . and above all writing. . . . To the King of Egypt came Theuth and revealed his arts . . . the bad points and the good. But when it came to writing Theuth said, "Here, O King, is a branch of learning that will make the people of Egypt wiser and improve their memories; my discovery provides a recipe for memory and wisdom."

Plato himself, to be sure, soon denies that literacy is an aid to wisdom or even to thinking. For it is by reason and the mind that people learn and know, according to Plato; and the inertness of writing, its inability to speak about itself and the intellectual dependency it nourishes, means for Plato a diminution in the capacity of reason. (The idea of the *cost* or the *disadvantages* of literacy is virtually unacknowledged in historical references to literacy since Plato—an absence that supports my suggestion of the euphemistic sense that has come to be attached to the concept of literacy.) Quite aside from the question of the cost of literacy, however, the account cited by Plato of the origins of literacy as an aid to memory has at least some historical support. The fragments of early writing to which we have access come most often under the rubric of an odd literary form, the genre of lists or catalogues: lists of lands, genealogies, posses-sions, supplies, acquisitions, battles. Such lists undoubtedly serve various functions,* but it is reasonable also to assume a common denominator— that they provide for their author or sponsor a means of access to what otherwise would be lost or mistaken. For an army that depends on stores of food and arms, it is obviously advantageous to have a compilation of what those supplies are; their enumeration in a list that exists indepen-dently of a particular person—in effect, a means of public memory— marks such an advance.

It is hardly necessary to labor this point or to multiply examples, for one can look almost randomly at current examples of writing to find evidence of their standing as forms of artificial memory: the codifications

---

* Is it too fanciful to think of lists as a form of narrative manqué? Only supply causal and chronological connectives, and lists turn into chronicles, and then narratives.

of laws; the compilations of individual and group history; the notations of experimental science. All of these presuppose a threefold means—of recording, preservation, and transmission—and those factors are exactly what literacy (although perhaps not only literacy) provides.

A second hypothesis concerning the function of literacy is rather more venturesome than the first, but not less pertinent. Levi-Strauss, in *Triste Tropiques*, links the origins of literacy to the hierarchy of political power—claiming in effect that, both originally and subsequently, the ability to read and to write has historically served as an instrument of social domination, of the enforcement of power structures. Evidence for this claim is apparent in these same examples of early writing that have been cited above. For even if we leave aside the power that mysteries exert of themselves—and thus also the power of anyone able to inscribe or decipher the texts of religious authority—the aid provided to functional memory even by the genre of lists also, at a later remove, turns out to be an important instrument of social control. It may seem only "natural" that the history of the spread of literacy in Western culture roughly parallels the history of those classes that hold power: these, we might surmise, have the leisure and the means to develop the skills of literacy. But what, Levi-Strauss asks, if the causal connection went in the other direction?— if literacy *provided* the ruling or dominant classes with a means of obtaining and retaining power, if it had something to do with the fact that they *acquired* power?

Again, these two hypotheses are just that—and there undoubtedly is counter-evidence to them individually as well as alternate hypotheses that would explain the same evidence. But what is significant about the explanations cited is that *some* such account is unavoidable. The institutions of a society might, as Borges proposes in "The Babylonian Lottery," come into existence by mere chance, as a consequence of the human will to play—but the odds of that (as for any lottery) are small indeed. Without reference to need and function, in other words, the institution of literacy becomes unintelligible—and this fact brings me to the main thesis of these comments. For if indeed literacy has a historical character, *in its origins,* there is every reason to believe that the same character would also govern its subsequent history and even, as it may occur, its end. To be sure, we know that the reason(s) *why* something comes into existence may not explain its continued existence; and it is clear that the history of literacy, especially since the Renaissance and the development of printing, with the accompanying proliferation of literary genres and the development of natural and social science, was not and could not have been anticipated in the origins of literate culture or of the very concept of literacy. But although, if the original need that produced literacy had now disappeared or if it were being met by other means than those which first responded to it, this would not necessarily make literacy obsolete, it would establish at least the possibility of obsolescence. Certainly, the details of that history would provide important information about the social transformations that those (or any) cultural needs and the responses to them might undergo.

And, of course, for the two hypothetical histories of literacy cited above, the displacement of the needs alleged to have produced those histories originally is in fact exactly what has *actually* taken place. The memory capacity of the computer and of other forms of artificial intelligence has so extended the already artificial memory of literacy as to make the latter seem primitive as a form of retention. The keeping of lists now can extend almost instantaneously into the tens of millions of items—and the language required for access to that memory is a radically simpler language than the written one of traditional literacy. More than this, the 'speaker' of computer languages easily serves many others who are themselves illiterate; like the masters in a society where slaves do the reading, there is no need for these others to duplicate in their own memories what the computer has in its memory or even to learn how to converse with it. The possibility that computers may require no special language but might be addressed orally and in "natural" language introduces only slight changes into this prospect.

We thus have to take seriously the possibility that as artificial intelligence itself becomes literate, the ideal of literacy as a human function, certainly as a cultural necessity, will simply become obsolete. "If I have a dog, why should I bark?" the English adage goes. The fact that machines can do a job as well as human beings, let alone better than they could, has long been seen as a reason why humans should not be asked to do the job at all. And again: literacy has now also been embodied in mechanisms of representation and transmission. To be sure, social power and control continue to include control of the traditional instruments of literacy—the newspapers, the publishing presses. But the balance has already swung away from these to devices much more closely related to the means prominent in pre-literate society, and especially to the human, non-linear image and voice. As that emphasis (in films, television, etc.) is joined with the interlocking informational and predictive networks of the machinery of computers and artificial intelligence—and with the power of social control that this combination conveys—we see how far we have already gone and, more than this, are yet likely to go, toward a post-literate society.

History, of course, can be wrong as well as right, and even the likelihood of the prospective change I have been describing would hardly be evidence of its desirability. One great problem with technological development, we know, is that by the time anyone has the opportunity to assess that development, it is very difficult to go back, to undo it—and if this is true generally, it has implications as well for the possibility of reviving literacy as a cultural (and realistic) ideal. When the president of the United States can say in response to a question about which books he has recently read, that he doesn't care for that sort of thing (this was Ronald Reagan, but it might also have been another), we are, however reluctantly, forced to admit that something is happening in the culture that may be bigger than any of us. At the very least, it brings clearly into the light important questions that had otherwise, in the mystification of literacy as inevitable or as an assumed cultural value, simply been obscured. We have long recognized within literature the evolving history of genres, and we ought now, under the pressure of technology, to begin to consider the possibility that literature itself, as a whole, is a genre in evolution. So, too, we can ask ourselves, not disinterestedly but with an immediate point, what the price is that has been paid for literacy, what possibilities of expression have been excluded by it, what the history of literacy has *cost* in terms of culture alone. And thus we also address a question to the future, about the possibilities that a post-literate culture may provide—in the way of art or science or a domain of spirit yet untouched. Only Pollyanna would be confident that the answers to these questions will be reassuring—but at least we should know better now than to recommend the features of our own culture as necessary or natural to all culture.

3

The Rights of Black English

At first glance, language may seem to have nothing to do with ethics, but I shall be claiming the contrary here—that far from our usual idea of language simply as a means or tool (like a hammer or spoon) which we then put to whatever use we choose, language, much like people, has its own character, and more specifically, an ethical character. It can indeed serve as a means to other ends, but it also affects those ends, and at times it stands for the ends themselves in the form of values or principles; like those ends, it too can be honest or deceptive, sincere or devious, democratic or authoritarian. Thus, language may act sometimes for the good, sometimes for evil—and *always* it is a form of action or doing, not a passive construct or "thing."

This proposal may seem only to add another problem to the many others evident in our subject. Aren't there difficulties enough, it might be asked, in ethical questions and in the concept of language by themselves without worrying about a connection between them? But if what I am saying is correct, we do not have a choice about this: the two *are* related, because of what they are and whether we like it or not, with the option left to us, then, only of discovering what this relation is, how it works. Although a connection between language and ethics may complicate certain questions, furthermore, it simplifies others. I hope to suggest in particular how it reduces the pressure exerted on the problem—the *alleged* problem—of Black English.

Consider first the idea of "correct" or "proper" or "right" usage in language—what people mean when they say, for example, that someone speaks or writes correctly. It is true that this and other related uses of the word *correct* seem often to be a kind of ethical judgment, pointing to what ought or ought not to be done: so, for example, we say that someone "behaved" correctly or incorrectly, meaning that the person did or did not do what he should have. Admittedly, good manners or etiquette (like using the "correct" fork) are only indirectly related to ethics; but we more often use "correct" not when we are talking about folkways or manners, but when we think that there is only one "right" way to do something and other ways of doing it that are not. So, for example, we add a column of figures: there's one correct answer here (we assume), and the others are wrong. And in general when we call a statement or expression correct, the model imposed is that of science, in the statements that a physicist or chemist or biologist might make about how different parts of the world work. To be sure, scientists, too, may turn out to be mistaken in what they claim—but whether they are or not, and *when* they are or not, we do not think of this as a matter of custom or manners: it's a matter of fact.

It is this, then—what might be called the "scientific" model of correctness—that we usually have in mind when we refer to the "correct" use of language when we teach students how to write, when we call their attention to "mistakes" in grammar, and so on. And although it is not difficult to understand why we define or apply the terms *correct* and *incorrect* in this context, we need to remind ourselves that this conception of "correct" usage in relation to language is itself not quite correct. To put the matter more bluntly, it is false. There are in fact two mistakes that this account makes—two hard (and related) facts that it starts out by ignoring and ends up contradicting.

The first of these hard facts is that language is historically rooted, a *part* of history. It had a beginning in history, even if it is one that scholars do not and probably never will know much about; it has developed and changed, broken up into pieces and reassembled in so many different and unpredictable ways that there is something misleading even in referring to language as an "it": the "it" is more probably a "they." Language and languages have never stood still—they seem always in motion, always changing. Admittedly, it is possible to *imagine* a language that does not change: this is one reason that mathematics has had such a strong and continuing appeal. *There,* we might agree, is a language outside of time; once true, always true. But people do not "speak" mathematics—even in classrooms, let alone when they eat breakfast with their families or when they argue about politics. And the languages they do speak at these times

26

seem historically always to be moving, to introduce new terms and meanings, and also to make certain idioms or phrases, aspects of style and even parts of grammar obsolete. But if languages are always changing in this way, then also the standards in those languages must be changing. And this means in turn that if we think of correct speaking or writing as following a set of laws from which any deviation is a mistake, we are mistaken. The laws themselves are constantly in the process of deviating from past laws; they themselves, in other words, break other laws. What is recognized as correct in speaking or writing at one time will not be at another, even in the same language, let alone in a different and foreign one.

Second: this pattern of change in the history of "correct" usage—in the history of grammar and vocabulary, and also in the style of language— is not (or at least not only) a natural history. It is not, in other words, akin to the process of growing in which, for example, whatever a child does, certain standard biological changes will take place in him or her over time. There may to some extent be an inner logic in the evolution of language, certain regular developments that turn one particular sound or grammatical practice into another—but it is still more certain that *decisions* play a role in establishing the standards of what is correct or not in a language, and that these decisions are made by speakers and writers within the society itself. I do not mean anything as extreme here as that every time we say or write something, we consciously consider whether to obey or to disobey a rule of language—but a version of this process does occur, one that becomes much sharper and more definite when multiplied by the great number of speakers and writers of the language who do the same thing. Examples of such quasi-decisions are numerous, and I mention only one to make the more general point. In all English grammar books published at the beginning of the twentieth century, a sharp distinction was defended between the words *will* and *shall*. In the simple future tense, these books instruct their readers to say that "I *shall* be going downtown tomorrow," but that, in the third person, "Jack and Elizabeth *will* be going downtown tomorrow." Precisely the reverse arrangement is required, however, if we are deciding, not just predicting or anticipating, what is going to happen: "I know you don't want me to, but I *will*

27

go downtown tomorrow anyway.'' Or, in the third person again: "Jack and Elizabeth *shall* go downtown tomorrow—or I'll know the reason why . . ."

Now in grammar books published in the 1980s, this distinction in the usage of "will" and "shall" is referred to (when it is mentioned at all) at most as an option; more often, it is not mentioned, and this suggests the strong possibility that by the end of the century or soon after that, the distinction will have disappeared altogether. Who decides this, and why? Well, those questions themselves may seem to be question-begging: are such changes really the result of decisions? But the alternative to that explanation would be the improbable possibility that the changes simply "happen." In any event, there are, we know, many different ways in which decisions are made. Just as we assume that the distinction between "shall" and "will" *first* came into the language because it had some use or value, so its disappearance would also be related to someone's (or some group's) view that it had outlived that use. In other words, there are *reasons* for changes in what is accepted as correct usage in language.

This may sound as if I am suggesting that the evolution of "correct" or "normal" usage is entirely a rational or practical process—one, furthermore, in which all the speakers or writers of a language share equally. But the history of usage demonstrates that neither of these is the case— not the rationality and not the equality. It is at this point in fact that the relation between language and ethics begins to show itself most clearly. If experience provides any lesson about how the rules or laws that govern people are made—whether they are legal rules or economic rules or, as here, grammatical rules—it is that social power is not evenly distributed, that some individuals and some groups in a society have more to say than others about what becomes the law or norm and so about what is accepted as correct behavior or punished as deviation. This imbalance or bias may or may not be an intrinsic feature of social organization; but it unquestion-ably has been a persistent feature historically—even, it has to be said, in societies which profess an ideal of equality among its citizens, as in the principle of "one person, one vote."

Speaking and writing are prominent examples of social behavior, and thus it is hardly surprising that a society, in its educational institutions but also in its other institutions, should put much emphasis on the question of what is correct or not in them. Nor is it surprising that a close connection should be discernible between what is generally accepted as correct usage and the patterns of speech or writing of the social groups or classes closest to the levers and wheels of power. One of the most striking examples of this connection appeared (and still remains, although to a lesser extent) in England—where the very accent in which a person spoke was a near-certain indicator of social class, at a time when membership in one class or another effectively determined the economic and social status of each person in the society (for better or, more often, for worse).

This thesis is both general and large, and I don't attempt to prove it here. But it is clear enough, even without such proof, that language, like other social institutions such as the legal system of a state or country, or the educational curriculum in the public schools, provides a ready means of social control, of organizing and regulating society. It can be used and has been used to keep some people out of power and to admit others; it establishes the presence of a voice of authority—an unelected one—to which speakers or writers then find themselves subject if, for example, they want to publish a book, or to get a job as a newspaper reporter or as a fireman or as a public school teacher.

I do not wish to seem here to move from one extreme to another—from objecting to the idea of ''correct'' usage as based on a form of scientific truth to the opposite view that would leave ''correct'' usage as not truthful at all but only an instrument of social control. The latter would imply that language as a whole is no more than a weapon in the struggle for power, whether by individuals or social groups—and although that is undoubtedly too close to historical truth for comfort, it also is an overstatement. We can avoid both extremes, however, by asking ourselves what language is good for at its best and irrespective of its origins: what we can reasonably *hope for* from language. It is here, it seems to me, that ethics links up directly with language—and points out something important about the particular status of Black English. The most common way of thinking about language is of language as descriptive, a form of representation: words stand for things or events and qualities or feelings which are then linked together in sentences or other pieces of discourse. And insofar as this representational function indeed holds for language, we then also know what the goal or result of the function is: statements which describe or represent parts of the world and of experience enable readers or listeners to conceive for themselves those aspects of the world or experience. Readers or listeners, in other words, think or imagine in their minds something close to what speakers or writers had first had in theirs.

Language at its best would in these terms represent accurately and without bias; it would be, the listener or reader could hope, truthful, honest, open, direct, sincere—not evasive or obscure or misleading. It would not in other words, *mis*represent or lie. But each of these terms, it is obvious, designates a moral or ethical characteristic; the terms as a group refer to qualities that we consider important in people's actions or characters as they are encountered in all the parts of everyday life, not only in speaking or writing. And once we recognize that these qualities figure also as values of language—in other words, that language is a way of acting, of doing things to other people (and at the same time to ourselves as well)—this gives a very different view of how language is to be evaluated from that proposed in the "scientific" conception of language. There is no longer a single linguistic standard of correctness; the assessment of writing or speaking is not based on how closely they follow certain rules, but how effective, how direct, how honest, how convincing they are—in short, how they do what language as such is meant to.

Consider the two following examples of usage as they exhibit this distinction between rules and effectiveness. The first example would be generally accepted as conforming to standards of "correct" or "normal" usage; it is part of an article about religion in a journal of sociology, and the two authors of the article are university faculty members: "Flooded by mass media with such a range of alternative prescriptions on how to live, and sensing that these alternatives are *not* all equally valid for them, some individuals will continue to seek in church affiliation a basis for ordering their personal priorities and for sustaining their beliefs that particular normative patterns are preferable" (M. I. Harrison and B. Lazerowitz, "Do Denominations Matter?" *Am. J. of Sociology* 88 [1982], p. 373). The second quotation is also about religion; it has the form of a prayer, in fact, in Black English, as quoted by Martin Luther King: "Lord, we ain't what we ought to be, and we ain't what we want to be, we ain't what we gonna be, but thank God, we ain't what we was."

By the standard of correct usage that the first quotation passes, the second one obviously fails: it makes a number of grammatical mistakes, joining a single predicate to a plural subject, and so on. On the other hand, if we apply to the two statements the *other* standards that have been mentioned, the ranking unmistakably goes the other way. For directness, clarity, precision, vividness, honesty—in other words, for writing as a means of expression: practical, ethical, artistic—the Martin Luther King statement is much more compelling, more vivid, more communicative, more of a *statement* than the other one. We (the audience) know exactly what it means or represents; we have a good sense of why it says what it does and what it wants from us in response, although it also leaves the audience the freedom of response. None of these is true for the first statement, which has the rhetorical effect mainly of putting the reader off, of establishing and maintaining a distance between reader and text. If the authors do not exactly wish to conceal the idea they express, they want to make sure that the reader knows how difficult that idea is; they hope then also to evoke a response from the reader that would acknowledge their authority over both the idea and the reader.

The question might still be raised, to be sure, of what these differences amount to. For it is still possible to claim, *has been* claimed, that for the different uses of language and of the ways people talk or write, there are no objective standards of judging, that all the varieties have equal claims if only because no person or group is in a position to judge among them. At the level of absolute justice, this claim has an obvious appeal; construed democratically, it would hold that there is nothing to choose between white and black or any other color of English, that all language and all uses of language are (quite literally) created equal. But this does not follow, and more importantly, at another level, it is obviously false. For one thing, there is a practical question at stake here. If the levers of social power are in the hands of people for whom "normal" usage is different from that of Black English, then this is a practical argument for learning the language that holds power simply *because* of its position as correct or normal. This again is a practical reason, not itself a moral reason; it might in fact be judged an immoral reason, since it proposes to use language merely as an instrument. (Notice that even this would not be a reason for not using Black English; it says nothing against dialects or bi- or tri-lingualism, with the evident advantages that these often have.)

31

And second and more importantly, the contrasting examples show, as clearly as the point can be, that differences in the effectiveness and quality of language are unmistakably there to be found—although not, certainly, by the "color" of the language. In these terms, language can—ought to—be judged as a means of expression: for its effectiveness, its imaginative force, its liveliness, its precision. Admittedly, there are no rules or laws that can be followed to achieve *these* goals (if there were, the sociologists who wrote the sentence quoted before would probably have followed them). But although there are no recipes for assuring a life to writing or speaking, the difference between words or texts that have those qualities and those that do not is almost always evident, certainly as evident and immediate and compelling as anything else in our experience. There may then be practical reasons why we should concern ourselves about the difference between Black English and the version of English that differs from it and is regarded as standard. But beyond this, or rather, below it and more fundamentally, there are even better reasons why we should first be concerned in relation to the language we speak or write with how effectively it does the work that language as such is intended to. Here we should be distinguishing not between normal or "correct" usage and Black usage—but between language that is alive, direct, responsive to its subject—and language that is not. And this is an issue, like any other important social and ethical concern, for all usage and for everyone equally. Finally, then, it is not Black English that is the problem, but English. Or, more precisely, language itself.

4

Anti-Anti-Obscenity

The past trials of Ulysses and Lady Chatterly and the present (1990) trials of the Mapplethorpe collection of photographs and of "rap" lyrics have successively failed to advance the question of how we—or anyone else— are to distinguish obscenity from art. Verdicts and proscriptions have been handed down, of course; but far from shedding light on this subtle problem of aesthetics, they seem rather by their own shapeless, often contradictory criteria to force the public affected by those judgments back to walking the rough ground of the maxim "De gustibus non disputandum est." Even, it might be added, when the "gustes" belong to the makers or the judges of a country's laws.

One could be grateful, perhaps, that the resources of a busy and preoccupied country should in whatever context be spent on discussions of philosophical questions. If obscenity starts where art ends, after all, we must have agreed before reaching that end on what art is. Indeed, in all the recent legal discussions concerning obscenity or pornography, the premise has been acknowledged that if the work in question *were* "art," then it would not be pornographic—at least, on balance. And while no very good reasons have been given to support this premise, its effect at least is to commend art as something whose value overrides uses of language and representation which society would not otherwise (publicly) countenance. Art, in other words, is taken to offer something more than the virtue of its defects.

But at least one question is consistently begged in these discussions of obscenity that makes the flame hardly worth the candle; this is the still more basic question of whether a legislature or a court, having found to its "satisfaction" that a book or photograph or song is obscene, ought even then to rule that nobody else in the state or city or country should be allowed to view or to hear it. Admittedly, reasons *might* be given for such constraints on moral or legal grounds—for example, that obscenity causally affects the behavior of its readers, as in a connection between the reading of pornography and certain crimes; or that obscenity is addictive, capturing unsuspecting viewers or readers and bending them to its will; or that by its diversion of interest and energy, it may exhaust the creative energies of a citizenry and thus threaten the viability of the country.

These are indeed reasons that have been used to justify other legal restrictions—those, for example, governing wartime censorship or the distribution of drugs; it would then at least be consistent if the case against obscenity rested on these or related grounds. But this is not how matters stand. Its most ardent enemies do not claim to have found *evidence* against pornography of the kinds mentioned—and the assumption that such evidence is there to be found is opposed by other assumptions which, at least until more facts are in, seem no less persuasive. Just how does the experience of obscenity or pornography affect its audience? What we find instead of an answer to this question are indictments and arrests made *as if* we knew—as if, moreover, we knew that the effects were pernicious not only for the individual directly involved, but for society as a whole.

It is not surprising that we should be ignorant of the effects of pornography on its audience when we know so little about the effects of literature or art more generally. To be sure, there is no shortage of *intimations* of morality: Plato's tirades (against, one must add, the misunderstanding of art), the claims of Shelley, Tolstoy, and even, if we strain the texts a bit, Aristotle and Kant—all affirm the moral consequences of art and the fact (albeit construed in various ways) that it works for good or evil on its audience. There is, of course, a dissenting side to this view which argues that in the encounter with art, readers or viewers ought properly to will the "suspension of disbelief," to detach themselves from the assertions or implications of art in a way that leaves them only formal possibilities and thus in end as morally irrelevant. But even if we assumed the former of these two positions, holding that literature is morally significant and thus may indeed at times be pernicious or morally culpable, we might still wonder that its "prurience" should be singled out for regulation from the assortment of other occasions or examples that have much the same effect but nonetheless pass unregulated and even unnoticed.

The shoe-fetishist, for example, does not have to be devious or even literate to find objects of prurient interest; and any man or woman is safe (protected by law) to consider and also to enjoy the sometimes obscene interest that passers-by may rouse. We single out books and photographs or "rap" groups, however, as objects for censorship; and the explanation usually given for this is that, unlike the other examples cited, they might be intended solely or primarily to arouse prurient interest. But even this distinction is invidious—and one has only to follow the cross-currents of our culture to recognize this. Prurience, after all, the stigma picked on most frequently in the attacks on pornography, refers in its first meaning to a longing or itch—the desire to satisfy an interest centered in the self and its pleasures. And then there come to mind the gratifications of the television soap opera and the film fantasies of power and success—or, more practically, the techniques of advertising which promise an inventive collection of satisfactions for the cost of a bar of soap or a box of cereal. Even the fictionalized non-fiction of such journalism—"news"—makes overtures of fantasy and pleasure to readers who are then left to elaborate on them privately and vicariously. Which of these forms of expression is not prurient? That some are more heavily disguised than others, far from detracting from this quality, intensifies it by the use of a veil. In common, they act as drugs for the varieties of social disease—isolation and rootlessness, the inanity of much everyday work—even more than they do as masks for sexual frustrations or anticipation.

The society we live in undeniably distinguishes sex and its fantasies from the others in the group, perhaps because the taboos surrounding sex are one of the few relics in an otherwise ill-stocked museum of traditions. The individual has the right, we agree, to choose a profession (if he or she can get the education) and to vote on the basis of conscience (if this can be fitted to the candidate). The law allows people to tell lies in their personal dealings and to be neurotically oppressive in other ways as well to acquaintances, relatives, "friends." They can fantasize about a life to come or a paradise lost, or choose to be as ignorant or bigoted as they wish about the world they inhabit. But they cannot, it seems, where obscenity stands at its source, follow their sexual musings even if the transaction involves nobody and nothing more than themselves and a book or a picture or a song.

Were the social dangers posed by these transactions really a matter for concern, surely the attempt should first be made to understand the conditions that foster them. For unless an interest in obscenity is assumed to be innate, a trait of human nature, there should be an explanation for it in the variable conditions (the repressions—or, perhaps, on the other hand, the creative impulses) that impinge on the more authentic and so non-prurient traits of human nature. Instead of doing this, however, those who war on obscenity and pornography move to excise the symptom, to purge desire. And this can be effected, it is clear, only as legal or social regulations are invited to legislate the emotional life of the individual even when it concerns the individual alone. Justification for this, it is clear, cannot be or at least has not been given on social grounds, but relies on declarations of principle or purity drawn from other sources—from a divine law or an a priori moral code ascribed to a society for which, officially, they do not exist. One would think that the twentieth century had had a surfeit of attempts to make people over into someone else's image of God.

The moral issue aside, one can mention as well the practical incongruities of censorship. To label a photograph or book obscene more often than not has the consequence only of increasing its circulation and price. The apparatus required to systematically enforce censorship regulations is unwieldy and constrictive; the analogies here are with cures that kill and babies going out with the bath water. How many policemen and jailers do we want? And this says nothing, to be sure, of the judges and legislators themselves, going home each night, as it must then be, briefcases straining with the provocative and the lurid, listening to music and visiting museums that will harm or damage them. Should we care less for their well-being than for our own?

It's too bad—probably—that people find (or feel obliged to find) gratification in obscenity. Better, no doubt, the reality than a surrogate; much better, obviously, to quarrel with the cause of a malady than with the symptom. But in the list of things that are "too bad," how bad is this? And when the punishment is harsher and more indiscriminate than the crime, how does one decide which is which? Notice that this view does not deny that certain books or photographs or lyrics may be obscene or pornographic (perhaps also, by that fact, not art). This possibility remains open and vague as the courts and the philosophers have left it—which is, we need no reminding, *quite* open and vague. The claim here is only that even if the distinction holds, and even if we agree that the label of obscenity or pornography applies, the members of a body politic who are responsible for its laws and for their own selves still have no answer for the rudimentary question, "So what?"

5

Politics and the New History of Truth

"What is truth?" Pontius Pilate asked skeptically, hoping for the worst, and would have found himself comfortably at home with presidential politics in the United States. The issue is not so much that presidents or the people they have appointed to office have been lying with increasing frequency and decreasing shame, but that they have revised the very concept of truth, in a series of changes that now almost obscure the distinction between lying and telling the truth altogether.

Philosophical disputes aside, in practical affairs almost everybody shares a definition of truth that is notably simple and clear if only because it is no more than the opposite of lying. As lying means asserting something not in accord with facts known to the speaker, telling the truth requires that the assertion reflect those facts or at least does not *not* accord with them. It would be difficult to find a schoolchild above the age of five who, at some level, is unaware of this difference, and indeed almost all the links that hold social institutions together—laws, contracts, promises, even simple descriptive statements—assume this very distinction.

The political imagination is unusually inventive, however, in the face of prohibitions or taboos, and a notable moment in the new history of truth occurred during the Nixon administration—not, again, with the straightforward and so, in a way, honest lies told by the president and his colleagues (to each other as well as to the rest of us), but more subtly with the concept of "deniability" that emerged in the Watergate trials as the Nixonians' working definition of truth. Where in common usage, the truth of a statement implies a correspondence with facts, including those that might be known only to the speaker, deniability ascribes truth to any statement that cannot be disproved: all claims to the contrary can then be "denied" (or, over a longer period, "stonewalled"). This definition has been especially useful for statements made by members of presidential

38

administrations since Nixon's about actions they had been responsible for but which, they believe, no one could trace to them. To be sure, the latter assumption sometimes has proved to be mistaken—but this is an error of calculation, not in applying the principle that anything asserted is true until disproved. One predictable consequence of this conception, of course, has been that government officers also feel justified in preventing access to evidence that might disconfirm what they had said. Such concealment would, in a perverse sense, be "right": without counterevidence, the original assertion remains "true"—and why *should* anyone collaborate in proving it false?

Again, this theory of truth is not simply a revised version of lying, not even a part of the requirement that telling the whole truth is somehow related to telling the truth. It means that the test of truth is now negative: all assertions—claims or denials of responsibility, descriptions of events— are true until they are disproved. If they are. The burden of proof is thus entirely on the audience and not at all on the speaker, whose main concern, once he has spoken, is to retain the power of deniability by assuring that possible counterevidence remains hidden.

The assertion "I can't remember," which during Watergate became virtually a formal instrument of government policy, epitomizes this first step in the redefinition of truth. It is possible, of course, to object that a faulty memory about important public matters should disqualify the person who has it, but it is almost impossible to *prove* that someone who says he doesn't remember something actually does remember it. This is, then, the principle of deniability at its most elegant.

But the times have moved beyond the inventiveness that went into the concept of deniability which still, at *some* point, concedes the indepen- dence of facts from what is said about them. The Reagan theory of truth moved a step toward denying the latter distinction altogether, replacing deniability as the standard of truth by what the Reaganites, with biblical irreverence, characterized as the "spirit" of the truth in contrast to the facts or evidence that might be thought to govern that spirit. Standing on this distinction, President Reagan, not only impromptu but also in his prepared speeches, presented a number and variety of statements as fact that were false and were soon shown to be. When these statements were challenged, subsequently, the response came from various presidential spokesmen that the "spirit" of the statements—what they exemplified or stood for—was true even if the particular examples or figures cited in the statements were not.

It seems reasonable to infer that if examples or figures that did support the "spirit" of the arguments had been available, they would have been cited. And we might reasonably conclude, then, that the "spirit" put to work here is *meant to* be independent of the facts, in short, that the facts— the number of welfare cheaters or mortgage foreclosures or ICBMs that we don't have—are governed by the policy being defended rather than the other way around. As a Reagan spokesman said about one statement of "fact" that the president had gotten wrong: it "might as well have been true."

A notable irony attaches to this last displacement in the concept of truth, since it suggests that there may be no truth (not even the circumscribed truth of "deniable" assertions) apart from their "spirit," that is, apart from the theories or ideologies that motivated the statements in the first place. The extremity of this claim is something that Marxists have long yearned for but have been wary of asserting because of a reluctant deference to at least some varieties of science and fact. The Reagan theory of truth, bound by no such scruples, thus out-ideologizes the Marxists. To speak in or with the "spirit" of political purpose is to determine the facts which then, unsurprisingly, turn out to support it.

George Orwell was only one of many writers to argue that corruption in a society or culture quickly discloses itself in the language; and the new history of truth described here has already disclosed itself, like a character in search of an author, in the term *misspeak*. So far as I can trace it, the current usage of that verb was first introduced by Ron Ziegler, President Nixon's press secretary, who had plenty of opportunity to misspeak (himself or others) in the weeks leading up to Nixon's resignation. In its early appearances, the term was used reflexively, implying that the speaker did the misspeaking *to* himself; this feature soon dropped out, however, and the term then came to be used in any person and intransitively (I misspoke, you misspoke, he or she misspoke). But this clarification of syntax does nothing for meaning, and the reason for this is that the term is *intended* to conflate two very different terms, each quite familiar and intelligible by itself.

The first of these is the word *mistake;* the second, *lie.* If in good faith I assert a statement of "fact" that later turns out to be incorrect, I have made a mistake. The mistake itself may be culpable (that is, perhaps I should have known what I didn't), but even so, I said what I said because I didn't know any better, and in this sense the *making* of the statement is not culpable. To lie is to present an assertion as true that the speaker believes to be false; he does know better but says it anyway. It is the considerable distance between these two that the term "misspeak" was meant to obscure, suggesting that what was said—misspoken—was a matter only of the speaking, as if the tongue somehow had acted by itself (like a gun when it misfires). The speaker is not simply mistaken—because that would suggest an innocence of intent or perhaps a lack of control that in the context is pretty obviously false and is in its own terms inconsistent with the image of presidential power and omniscience; on the other hand, what he says is not a lie—even venial or white—because presidents (or their spokesmen) don't do that or at least don't admit to that even when the evidence is unmistakable. The term itself thus breaches the law of non-contradiction, at once implying and denying that what was said was said intentionally. In practical terms it is another way of denying responsibility for telling the truth. The claim is especially insidious since it also suggests, as the new history of truth does more generally, that aside from the telling, there is no truth at all.

6

Pronouns and Affirmative Action

Disagreements about the ends, let alone the means, of affirmative action have divided both its friends and its antagonists, but there is a consensus even in these differences about the principle itself. Programs of affirmative action, it is agreed, are intended to work toward equality for members of groups which have suffered harm as the result of racial, ethnic, or gender discrimination based on that group identity. The questions of how the goal of social equality is to be achieved (or, for that matter, how it is to be measured), and who is to pay the inevitable costs for doing this, continue to pit the supporters against the critics of affirmative action (and sometimes each of these against themselves). Yet overriding those disputes is a common acknowledgment of the inequalities themselves, which are too obtrusive to ignore and too compelling to deny: in the workplace with its sharp discrepancies in status and income among racial or ethnic groups and between men and women; in family roles and in educational opportunities; and most urgently, although also most difficult to redress, in such rudimentary social facts as the numbers that measure life-expectancy and infant mortality.

The scale and extent of these inequalities make it understandable that most proposals for redressing them have been institutional, relying on legislative means. Thus, too, the concerns for economic and civil justice expressed by affirmative action programs have focused on groups rather than individuals, and it is undoubtedly true that without intervention by government—that is, if the matter had been left to individuals alone—even the modest gains so far realized by programs of affirmative action would be slighter than they have been.

This institutional emphasis, however, has diverted attention from the fact that it is a moral and so personal directive that at their source motivates programs of affirmative action, based on a conception of how certain people have as individuals treated—and by contrast, *ought to* have treated—others. Although we do not often hear about *personal* affirmative action programs, then, it is indeed at the level of the individual that affirmative action even in its institutional and seemingly impersonal appearances begins and ends, and at this level, too, that its rights or wrongs ought to be assessed.

This personal and moral group for the ideal of affirmative action is especially pertinent to one form of social practice which, although not without institutional features, is more obviously related than are most other practices to the acts of individual persons. In it both the consequences of past prejudice and the means by which affirmative action proposes to redress them are also evident. Those means are more easily available in this form of social practice than they are elsewhere since they involve none of the mechanisms that (however justified) have been sources of contention in many affirmative action plans: no quotas, no preferential weighting of candidates, no special allocations of funds. The candidate for affirmative action I have in mind here is language—more specifically, English—and I call attention to it in this context for the same reason that affirmative action programs are invoked elsewhere: because its "practice" (that is, the conventions of language) has come—willingly and wittingly or not—to incorporate prejudice and its effects, in many of the same forms that have appeared in other settings.

This general claim is no less familiar than the particular instance of prejudice that frames the discussion here; namely, the assumption in English of a hierarchy of genders in which (unsurprisingly, given the history of both hierarchies and genders) the masculine and its referent, men, have been privileged to the disadvantage of the feminine (that is, of women). This feature of "standard" English hardly requires much argument. An unusual epitome (unusual even among epitomes) will suffice; this is in the common use of the noun *man* (or *men*) as a synonym for *people* or *human beings*—that is, as referring to both men and women in the "gendered" sense of those terms. There could hardly be a more naively open or self-deconstructing statement, for instance, than the honored affirmation that "all men are created equal." To be sure, we are now given to understand in defense of this assertion that in it the term "men" refers not to a gender but to a genus; what it means is that "all *people* are created equal." But for one thing, although we may now accept this gloss (because with it—and only with it—the claim becomes morally compelling), the evidence is strong that the assertion did not originally have that meaning.

The Declaration of Independence in which it appeared, and the other political credos that soon followed it, were unwilling to proscribe a variety of then-current laws or practices which implied that women were in certain respects quite *un*equal. If the declaration wished to include women among those judged to be equal—that is, as "men"—the change in status required for this would have warranted mention. Furthermore, and more pertinently for the present: although on reflection we might *decide* that in the familiar statement, the term "men" does or should mean "people" or "human beings," this decision itself requires time and interpretation as well as an effort to persuade others of this. And the need for these is itself an impediment to the equality supposedly being declared—all the more so, since one plain reading of the statement does not yield that conclusion at all.

Because even ordinary language has extra-linguistic consequences (social, psychological, moral), statements about social, psychological, or moral issues will still more emphatically entail such consequences. A notable example of the way that gender distinctions in language are made and unmade appears in the difference between gender and genus recognized in the respective meanings in classical Greek of the words "aner" and "anthropos." When Aristotle, for example, wrote his sweeping judgments of human nature—"Man is by nature a political animal," and "All men by nature desire to know"—he used the term "anthropos" (man, the genus), not "aner" (the gendered or masculine man). In other words, he not only meant but *said* "people." There is more than irony in the fact that it is the translation of those statements into English that obscures a distinction Aristotle himself reiterated, conflating those two quite different terms into an at best ambiguous one. The fault in the two statements quoted from the *Politics* and the *Metaphysics,* then, is not with Aristotle (who otherwise did, admittedly, endorse a hierarchy of the genders), but with his translators or, as they might hope to spread the blame, with the conventions of standard English.

It is no more possible now to revise the wording of "all men are created equal" in the Declaration of Independence than it is to rewrite Lincoln's address at Gettysburg in which, with the struggle of the Civil War adding weight to its meaning, Lincoln reaffirmed that commitment. But the prejudice high-mindedly exemplified in these two settings persists, less dramatically and no doubt less high-mindedly, in other still current norms and uses of English as well. And here at least, that is, *now,* a personal version of affirmative action is possible, directed against the linguistic conventions in terms of which one gender is given what by standards of equity would be more than its—that is, his—due.

Among the ways in which gender prejudice or hierarchy has become normative in standard English, none has been so widespread or persistent as its influence on the lowly pronoun—a part of speech whose very name suggests a subordinate role but which, no doubt abetted by this guise of humility, has risen well above that station. On their normal use, pronouns, we know, replace or "stand in for" nouns. Thus, in the sentence "Ann found the book she was looking for in her room," "she" and "her" replace "Ann" and "Ann's" respectively—terms which *could have* been used in the sentence but which would have made the sentence unwieldy, repetitive, and even ambiguous (there would be no assurance that the first Ann mentioned was the same as Ann-2 or Ann-3). The pronouns replacing the two nouns thus economize in the sentence; they also make clear that the first Ann is also the one who found the book and whose room is referred to, and they indicate as well, of course, that the Ann mentioned is indeed female.

Pronouns (here or elsewhere) accomplish these ends, moreover, through the use of a small number of simple words—itself a sharp contrast between them and the nouns they replace, as nouns look continually for ways to call attention to themselves, hoping to stand out in the crowd even when others there do have names of their own and still more invidiously when the others are lumped together in indiscriminate reference to such nouns as "things" or "places." In the scramble for status among nouns, moreover, "proper" nouns come in first; by contrast, there *are* no "proper" pronouns, except marginally perhaps with the always equivocal "I" or the royal "we"—both of them, after all, indefinitely transferable.

In inflationary times, then, pronouns offer substantial economies. But this should not blur the fact that these savings, too, come at a price, and one item of evidence for this is in the gender prejudice that pronouns, more than any other part of speech, have come to incorporate. It is not obvious why pronouns in particular should be guilty of this: that there are fewer pronouns than there are other parts of speech might make the categories by which we distinguish them more noticeable, but would not itself account for the forms that the distinctions take. In any event, the evidence of pronoun-prejudice is unmistakable, most noticeably in the conventions according to which the masculine pronoun is authorized to replace singular nouns or other pronouns of indeterminate gender. "Any writer worth his salt will recognize this rule"—we might bluster onward here, at once exemplifying both the practice and the problem.

To be sure, the "his" in this one example might be understood as a reflection only that writers in disproportionate numbers have *been* "he's", or that men, more than women, have earned "salaries." To this extent, the prejudice disclosed in the usage may not be only or even primarily linguistic. But also at work here is the linguistic convention according to which "his," although masculine in the sense of gender, is in another sense also proposed as gender-neutral, designating writers as such, male or female. It is not *mere* prejudice that the sentence exemplifies, then, but it is prejudice nonetheless. There would be nothing grammatically incorrect in saying, "Any writer worth his or her salt . . . ," although even if we ignored the jangle by which this displaces the original cliche, the clumsiness of "his or her" or "her or his" would remain. To be sure, the latter objection, raised in the name of simplicity or brevity, is not a justification for using the masculine pronoun alone. But it does raise an issue, and the same constraints apply to many other examples—to the rule of baseball, for instance, that would then go, "Three strikes on the batter, and he or she is out."

Again, the possible objection to substituting "he or she" in such examples would not—could not—be that the cumbersome addition is grammatically mistaken. One might conclude in fact that the awkwardness of adding "or she" or "or her" wherever "he" or "his" are supposed now to suffice is a symptom of the problem, not a reason for denying that the problem exists. But the usage is clumsy in many of its likely uses—and the same verdict is no less pertinent when the additional phrase appears in the aftermath of other pronouns like "everyone" or "everybody," which also have taken a singular—and so the masculine—pronoun ("Everyone has his own way of doing things"). Here, too, the more judicious "her or his" might replace "his"—and if that were the only alternative to the masculine pronoun, even its awkwardness there as elsewhere ("Each to his or her own . . .") might not be a good reason for avoiding it. There is in any event no reason to assume that equality in language, more than equality elsewhere, will come without exacting a price.

Other alternatives do exist, however, and although none of them seems to be without some disadvantage, the general failure in the past even to consider them seriously suggests that an indifference to linguistic meaning has accompanied prejudice in the choices of standard usage—a willingness to barter economy for values without even looking for a middle ground that might preserve both. These other possibilities provide specific examples of ways in which affirmative action might be applied to language; notwithstanding other differences among them, one intention is common and evident in them all, that is, to undermine or subvert linguistic conventions of gender that had held previously.

In pursuing this goal, some of the proposed alternatives go to the opposite extreme—as though to achieve equality by adding the same imbalance to the other side of the scale. The most common version of this alternative is the direct substitution of "her" or "she" where the masculine "his" or "he" appeared before. So, for example, Richard Rorty, who rejects on behalf of "liberal irony" the prejudice of foundations or fixed principles in language and everywhere else, writes that the "ironist" whom he commends must meet three criteria: "(1) she has radical and continuing doubts about the final vocabulary she uses . . . ; (2) she realizes that argument phrased in her present vocabulary can neither underwrite nor dissolve these doubts; (3) insofar as she philosophizes about her situation, she does not think that her vocabulary is closer to reality than others. . . ."

There is no reason to believe that Rorty regards "ironists" as typically female. But his use here of the feminine pronouns by themselves has the immediate advantage of economy over "she or he"; by parodying (in part because he repeats) the bias he criticizes, moreover, he also forces attention to the long-time convention that he means to subvert. Like most writers who use this locution, Rorty does not speak explicitly about the usage itself; there is no way of knowing, then, whether he intends it as a one-time practice (elsewhere in the same book, in fact, he employs the conventional masculine form), as a permanent and inclusive "rule," or—between these two—as a linguistic means enlisted temporarily, perhaps until the inequality that he is reacting against has been redressed.

It is worth noting as a general consideration that, conceptually, programs of affirmative action were at least initially *intended to be* temporary, on the premise that the inequalities they proposed to correct are not intrinsic but the result of social obstructions arbitrarily set in the past. The immediate advantage that affirmative action provides is meant to correct for the effects of this discrimination, which also, presumably, has been or will be ended. Once the institutional prejudice and its effects from the past have been overcome—and here particular issues like linguistic practice will be judged in the larger context of social equality as such—affirmative action would no longer be necessary: everyone would be setting out from approximately the same starting place with approximately equal access to institutional means and thus with no need for recourse to special dispensations. Like any remedy or form of therapy, in other words, the ideal of affirmative action is to make itself superfluous.

On this provisional conception of affirmative action, recommendations for permanent revision, as in the conventions of language I have mentioned, may seem out of place. But the short-term changes these would justify and the long-range goal of equality that motivates them are in the end inseparable. In any event, proposals that do not embody the "final cause" or goal of affirmative action in the changes they recommend would be worse than useless. In this sense, permanent solutions to the evidence of prejudice are closely tied to recommendations for change in the short run; and indeed virtually all the alternatives that have been proposed to the normative and masculine form of pronouns are designed to serve both those purposes.

So, for example, one such possibility would substitute plural pronouns (often already used this way colloquially) for singular ones. In "Everyone should do *their* own thing," for instance, "their" has the advantage over either "his" or "her" of being indeterminate (or inclusive) in respect to gender. Linguistic historians have supported this alternative by pointing out that historically, into the nineteenth century, the plural usage here was in fact grammatically acceptable. The latter argument itself, however, is two-edged—since if the criterion applied is that of practice, then current norms (which in this case reject the plural form) would have at least as strong a claim as any other. Furthermore, in some contexts the plural replacement is clumsy at best ("Each to *their* own . . ."); in others, it is confusing or worse ("A writer sometimes confuses *their* reader when *they* use a plural pronoun to replace a singular noun").

A second alternative that has been proposed involves the introduction of neologisms that avoid gender prejudice by defining new singular pronouns of indeterminate gender. In contrast to "him" or "her," such coined words would disclose nothing of gender—for example (as they have been suggested), by the evenhandedness of "shin" or "hir." But the prospects for all neologisms are shaky at best; and although advocates of this alternative might point to success in other efforts (for instance, as Ms. has moved toward parity with Mr.), none of the proposals for singular, gender-neutral pronouns has found even minimal acceptance. The written formula "s/he," although it is evenly balanced and meets other conditions for singular pronouns, affords no help with the other combinations that are required ("his or her" and "him or her")—and the term itself, of course, is impossible to *say*.

One possible solution has occurred to me that would at once retain the discursive economy of pronouns, observe the grammatical conventions, and in principle at least reach equality in the genders of personal pronouns. This would be to have each speaker or writer use his or her own gender—consistently employing the feminine "she" or "her" or the masculine "he" or "his" wherever a singular pronoun is needed to replace an indeterminate noun or pronoun. Men would then hold "each to his own," women "each to her own," with all such statements disclosing the writer's gender not as pertinent to what is said but as a matter of course—itself, after all, an implication of equality. (There are various linguistic precedents for such usage, for example, in Hebrew, where the speaker's gender, even when indeterminate in the "I" of the subject, is then specified in the verb form. Why should verbs reveal gender when pronouns do not? For the same reason, I suppose, that in English pronouns might when verbs do not.)

This proposal is open to the objection, admittedly, that it would not bring the female voice into contexts of discourse where the masculine forms have tended and may continue to dominate. But not every effort of affirmative action can correct all the conditions that warrant it—and it may be useful in any event to have a glimpse of what grammatical life would be like when affirmative action was no longer needed. (A more conscientious response to this objection might require male speakers or writers to use the feminine pronouns and female speakers or writers the masculine ones—a measure, it could be argued, of Dantesque justice, although (one also has to say) probably no more likely to be realized in this world than Dante's other finely weighted punishments.)

A rather different objection applies to the alternative cited earlier, in connection with the passage from Rorty's book, in terms of which singular feminine pronouns alone would replace indeterminate nouns or pronouns as a permanent and not only a provisional solution; that is, to continue to use "she" or "her" wherever a singular pronoun is required to replace an indeterminate term. This alternative could perhaps be defended under the heading of compensatory damages—one of the justifications sometimes given for affirmative action programs in general. But quite aside from the serious questions that might be raised about this as a justification, there is a practical issue as well about the mark it would leave. At the very least, privileging the feminine pronoun as a linguistic "monument" to past abuse invites the question by which all monuments are judged—what will it mean, or do, in the future?

None of these proposals, then, is free of difficulties; all of them, moreover, are prescriptive—against the historical evidence that linguistic conventions have in general gone their own way, indifferent to prescription and sometimes to conscience; like dictionaries, grammar books follow, rather than precede usage. To be sure, *some* prescriptions have been effective (although more often in technological than in expressive changes—as in the replacement of the Arabic by the Roman alphabet in Turkish). It may be, furthermore, that as consciousness of the need for a solution grows, this pressure will itself produce a consensus. Or it may be that the desire for consensus is itself beside the point: the ideal of uniformity in linguistic usage and orthography has gained a firm hold on writing and speaking in English mainly during the past two centuries, certainly more in that time than it ever had before, including earlier periods that contributed notably to English letters notwithstanding (or perhaps because of) the linguistic heterodoxy of those periods.

If, however, there is uncertainty about the direction that an affirmative action program for pronouns should take, there can be little about the problem that requires them: the role of bias or prejudice—inequality—in the linguistic conventions, and so also the importance of an awareness of that presence. If the alternative solutions for the future of pronouns described here no more than called attention to the practice they criticize, disclosing how unconscious and "natural" that practice has been, they would still be pertinent—not least as a demonstration of how values (and prejudices) shape language, even for its uses that do not seem to involve values at all. The effort to replace inequality with equality in linguistic practice does not imply an ideal of language as value-free; it insists only that since values will *in any event* affect linguistic norms, they ought to be values that we choose and are willing (and able) to take responsibility for. In this sense, language is a form of moral action—with writers and speakers its agents.

It might be objected that even an egalitarian formula for pronouns or for language more generally would not do much for affirmative action where it counts most—in producing equality in economic and educational opportunity, for example. And in fact there has been little in the way of tests or measurements to prove that gender prejudice in language is also likely to cause or increase prejudice in its users or audience in other settings. But the absence of such evidence might well demonstrate only that the effects of language are complex, rather than that no such effects occur. A similar, more flagrant impasse appears, after all, in what should be much less problematic settings—in confirming the differences, for example, between a "classical" and a vocational education, or more concretely, in comparing the social or even the intellectual differences in consequence of reading Agatha Christie and reading Shakespeare. We do, of course, *assume* differences in these contrasting pairs—but we also have to admit that this remains largely an assumption, reflecting a present ideal rather than past evidence.

Prejudice, the personal or institutional assertion of inequality among equals, is prima facie wrong—wrong as a matter of principle and thus even apart from the consequences that follow from it. When the Supreme

51

Court ruled against segregated schooling (in *Brown vs. Board of Education*, 1954), the Court did not deny that segregated schools could have high standards, or that schools on the two sides of the line might have equally rigorous programs: the fact of segregation itself was judged prejudicial. There is no supreme court for the linguistic practice of English; where such courts exist (as in the French Academy), they seem more a curiosity than a power, and the explanation for this is straightforward: the institution of language is moved by individual speakers and writers who thus take on the combined roles of legislature and judiciary. This fact makes the goals of affirmative action as applied to language at once less readily asserted (since there is no independent authority) and more accessible, since the goals depend on what individual speakers or writers do, beginning with us ourselves.

In a society where gender prejudice is evident to anyone able to recognize it at all—in the workplace, in political, intellectual, and religious institutions—the ideal of equality that reveals and then criticizes its deformation in those other settings warrants the same response to its violation in language. Language as a system of symbols is undoubtedly more arbitrary in the designation of its symbols than other such systems. But here, too, we recognize that the consequences of symbols are much more than only symbolic. ''What ends as grammar,'' Nietzsche explained this, ''always begins as rhetoric''—and so for grammar as for rhetoric we should not be surprised to discover a moral ground.

II Rewriting in the Academy

7

Academics and the English Language

When Rhetoric is put out at the door it comes in at the window.
—Morris Croll

By "academic writing" I mean the writing done by academics (as well, by implication, as the writing they do not do). What I shall be saying about that writing does not apply to all of it, nor does it apply to the academic fields equally. For one thing, I am concerned with writing in the "humanities," not, except by way of comparison, with the social or natural sciences—and, in the humanities, with the examples and derivatives of the "monographic method" which, in Lukács' words, first obscures the horizon of the problems it addresses and ends (I shall argue) by mistaking its own identity. That method recurs among the full-length works published in the humanities; it figures still more prominently among the essays, notes, and reviews in journals which are the bulk of academic writing and in which the later, full-length works—almost always collections: personal anthologies—usually make their first appearance.

We need not be inhospitable to the variety in these textual forms to recognize in them the traces of an unhappy consciousness: neither the authors—often writing under compulsion, little of it their own—nor their readers, bound to find a warrant for what *they* will soon write, nor a willingly indifferent public, content to ignore the continued making and offering of books, show signs of the personal commitment or eros that tradition has found at the origin of the search for wisdom. We see in such writing at best the product of a cottage industry: craftsmanlike, with the uneven and sometimes evocative edges of homespun, but always marked by the purpose of exchange, an economic means. At its worst, it carries the stamp of the assembly line: technologically codified, indifferent to questions of how it came to be produced or what purpose it was meant to serve. It might well, like other commodities, have sworn an oath never to give itself away.

This lament, to be sure, is not novel; it has been heard often enough to constitute by itself a literary genre resembling the older Jeremiad. It is, moreover, as likely to come from the writers themselves (when they are not writing) as from the members of their absent audience asked to explain why they are not reading. But the need is evident in response to this deprecation (self- and other-), to understand how practice can be so unaffected by conscience: why the moral commitment that all writing entails (and writing about moral commitment more certainly) should be purposefully denied. The inhumanities, we might well name the topics that these writings circumscribe (and often circumlocute); we need no surer evidence of how man can be a wolf to man—himself included.

The symptoms of the malady afflicting academic writing may seem in themselves benign, and undoubtedly they *would* be benign if the symptoms were not also the disease. The first and most evident of these symptoms takes the form of stylistic impersonality and uniformity—an effect which lays the ground for a game called "Name-Shuffle." *Rules of the Game:* Read the essays in any issue of an academic journal; then cut out the authors' names. Shuffle the names and reattach them randomly. What improbability results? Would it be a surprise to discover that one author under different names had written all the essays?

A second symptom ("Author's Elbow"?) measures the distance between the technical vocabulary or jargon flourished in academic writing and the English language as it is used non-professionally—as writers aim their words at other persons rather than at an abstracted skill or competence. *Rules of the Game:* Underline all the nouns and verbs in a single paragraph from any essay in an academic journal. Then collect ten professors from *other* "fields" in the humanities. Offer them the following wager: a nickel reward for every underlined word that *they* then use correctly in new sentences of their own making, a dime penalty for every word misused. (If you hear complaints about the uneven odds, remind the plaintiffs that you are asking them questions about English, their own lingua franca.) Contribute your profits to the Community (of scholars) Chest.

A third symptom might be named, as after a Pilgrim maiden, "Purity of Context''; it marks the indifference of academic writing to the way what is being written about matters to the historical setting either of the subject written about or of anything else. *Rules of the Game:* List ten questions, the first five of which you take to be the most important questions that face a person living today. For the last five, list the questions you would most like to have answered in the area of study of which a text you choose is part. Then make two measurements: (*A*) How many of your questions are even tacitly present in the text? (*B*) How many of your questions does the text *claim* that it addresses? Results: *B* will invariably be less than *A*—and both numbers will be very low.

To be sure, not everyone will agree that the symptoms named indicate a disease at all. In scientific rhetoric and method, in fact, they stand as virtues rather than defects. As we see how those items serve the method of science, moreover, we may also understand why the rhetorical model used by science has appealed so strongly to writers in the humanities. This borrowing is the source, I should claim, of the mistaken identity that afflicts the humanities: the very success of science has opened a flaw, moral as well as rhetorical, in its imitators.

So, for example: On the rhetorical model of science, it is crucial that what is asserted can be acted on and duplicated by any reader of the scientific text. Far from being a defect, then, neutrality in tone is a requirement; where it does not exist, the reader has the additional chore of distinguishing the line of argument from the imprint of the writer's individual voice or persona. The reader (and knowledge itself) is best served by facts displayed impersonally, unmarked by their past; it is the obligation of the writer to shape the facts to that understanding. The result of this collaboration is a text that has for a face only the corporate and impersonal features of science as a whole. The identity of the author may still be important as a means for social (or anti-social) conventions: Nobel Prizes, letters to the editor, claims of precedence; but not because it verifies what a knowing reader would have discerned in the physiognomy of the text.

The appeal to technical vocabulary in writing in the humanities similarly recalls the devices of scientific prose. Partly because of its drive for generality, partly because of the passivity ascribed to its objects (a passivity required if the objects are to be fully manipulated), science has fostered specialized languages designed to make explicit the structures of those objects. The most obvious characteristic of such artificial languages is their denial of a lived past: the makers of language think to start fresh, free of the dross of history, of metaphors (dead or alive), of rhetorical conventions. Language, on this account, is a window pane, framing in words what the viewer who looks through the window may then see in fact. Whoever speaks the language, furthermore, is unlikely to question the legitimacy of its innovation. A magical power accompanies the coining of words, and their retelling acquires the potency of ritual or prayer. The words themselves bring objects to life: no small part of the allure of artificial language is the sense in its creators that they are also the creators of the objects that they name.

The third point of analogy follows the boundaries that science observes between a particular job of work and the process of which that work is part. Intelligibility, we are asked to believe, is a function of parts as well as of wholes, if only because any part may itself appear as a whole. Modern science has rejected the notion of "final" cause according to which natural occurrence is affected by future purpose as well as by past condition; there is consistency then (the kind of consistency honored by the boy who found reassurance for the pair of socks he was wearing—one brown, one blue—in the fact that he had a similar pair at home) in the claim that the rhetoric as well as the practice of science should regard facts as given and discrete, rather than emergent or cumulative. As the natural world is populated by the objects named by formulas—atomic numbers, genetic codes—the scientist can hardly be faulted for conjuring an image which in its own structure mirrors that discreteness. The conception of truth displayed in this image presupposes that the objects of knowledge exist piecemeal, exhibiting no intrinsic or prospective connection. The discourse of science readily applies that conception to nature as a whole no less than to its parts.

These features of scientific writing and method have come to be accepted, even assumed, although this does not mean that they are acknowledged: the possibility that scientific writing has a more substantial character than that of a simple transparency threatens the claims of science over its objects. To be sure, the impulse behind this willed denial is understandable. Science, we know, has worked; whatever the blindness of scientific rhetoric, then, it has not stood in the way of practical results, and we might thus deny the presence of a medium altogether. But an alternative account would hold that science has been successful precisely *because* of its rhetorical means; the claim that its rhetorical form is among the technological accomplishments of science is more than only a possible irony. One measure of this genealogy is evident in the fact that the rhetoric of science now passes unobstrusively for the expression of common and good sense.

These points of analogy between the writing of science and writing in the humanities do not in themselves explain why the humanities have modeled themselves on scientific rhetoric—a question that evidently impinges on both social and intellectual conditions. It is clear, for one thing, that this miming at the level of discourse is related to professionalization at the level of practice in both the sciences and the humanities—an important feature in the recent sociology of knowers and knowledge; it almost certainly reflects the isolation of "disciplines" in the university (why not speak, instead of departments, of the *com*partments of English, history, philosophy?)—the institution at which advances have been mainly effected in both the sciences and the humanities during the past two hundred years. These related developments have argued for autonomy among the areas of knowledge, symbolizing the divisibility of any item of knowledge into discrete units. They have also provided a warrant for unending specialization: why, if distinctions are good, should we ever stop making them?

This account is perhaps too simple, but evidence that the rhetoric of the humanities has imitated the rhetoric of the sciences is substantial nonetheless—and with that the form of a false analogy, the case of mistaken identity: the humanities try to be what they are not, to do what they cannot. Karl Kraus wrote that psychoanalysis turned out to be the malady it was intended to cure—and so, it seems, by considerable effort and self-denial, the accomplishment of academic writing in the humanities. At times there may be good reasons why the invitation "Know thyself" should be declined. When Levi-Strauss, a dominant figure in recent humanistic thinking, can write that "the goal of the humane sciences is not to constitute man but to dissolve him," both man and the humane sciences may well acknowledge that they are in trouble.

The theoretical presuppositions of scientific rhetoric, it thus turns out,

59

also reveal the commitments that bind its imitators. The conception, for example, of a writer who claims detachment from what he is writing about implies that the objects of knowledge are unaffected by the process of knowing: the writer stands to one side; his objects, to the other. The act of writing is subordinate, then, to what is written about; no exterior (let alone ulterior) motives live on in the process of writing which then turns out to be ahistorical, its conclusions set outside of time. Apparent individuality in the writer or distinctness in his interest is appearance only—a deviation from the corporate process which is concerned mainly that the corporation itself be served.

The use of a special or technical vocabulary is meant to confer neutrality on what is being expressed and, behind that, on the writer. The goal of this usage is precision, the avoidance of nuance or impression—an ideal which presupposes that the objects represented are correspondingly precise and insular. Literary figures like metaphor or metonymy characteristically evoke associations that are singular, probably untranslatable, and that can be neither disputed nor verified; this opens the way to alternative interpretations, even to claims for intrinsic indeterminacy in the text interpreted. Science, by contrast, measures its success by measurements: formulas, relations, predictions—and although the units of measurement may be conventional, they are not likely to be mistaken for metaphors. Scientific assertion purports to be translatable into terms of practical verification; this implies that the manner or style of assertion is only ornamental. Factual content, the holder of a universal passport, easily crosses stylistic boundaries, and any obtrusion of style thus becomes a ground for suspicion. The ideal of contemporary scientific prose is of a form of writing from which style is altogether absent.

A related feature of scientific writing is the concept of truth by which it evaluates the claims of science and even its own means. Since the natural world is held to consist of discrete items, and since writing about that world ought then to mirror the same distinctions, trugh becomes a function of the (discrete) relations in which fact and description meet; any such relations is equal in that respect to all others. Furthermore, as propositional truth is the determinant value of discourse, no other versions of truth apply to individual statements or even to the whole (which appears then as a complex or conjugated individual); other possible criteria, like symbolic or representational truth, can only obscure the view of the discrete units. The fragmented world reveals itself accurately in the fragments of truth; a whole which the fragments compose is no more than a conglomerate—and so, also, for its value.

The category of the "humanities" is itself vague, of course, in respect to the specific "fields" that it includes as well as to their common features. If anything is clear about that category as applied to the work of history, literature, and philosophy, it is the centrality in it of the person— not as a member of a larger class of "things" (as in physics) or, in the other direction, as a candidate for reduction (as by chemical analysis), but as the primary unit of discourse. To be sure, writing in the humanities need not directly translate everything into this denominator—but nothing in such writing would be intelligible without the possibility: history, addressing the image of the person *as* historical being (both historian and "object"); the study of literature which focuses on representations of the self in the literary work and, from the outside, with its regard for literature as human expression; philosophy as it cuts the patterns of metaphysical structure to fit a concept of human nature (exhibited first, of course, in the philosopher's own person). In expositions of "natural" history the scientist, too, runs up against the challenge of human measurement; but the difficulty encountered here is in seeing how a "theory of bodies" can account for the movement of a single body (perhaps of human proportions), not how laws of motion might be inferred from a theory of human nature.

The element of discourse thus proposed for the humanities—the self as self—may seem at best vague, at worse, tautological. But attempts to apply the contrasting rhetorical model of science to humanistic questions have demonstrated, by the distortion of those questions, the incongruity of that model for human subjects. If, for example, the relation of the self to the means of expression is an unavoidable issue in historical or literary or philosophical discourse, writers who represent themselves as detached from their subjects mislead the reader (and probably themselves)—not only because everything they say is unavoidably partial, but because what they then write must itself contradict the writers' representation of themselves in the writing. What (or whom) they write about is not simply there to be written about; the writers *choose* to write about it, and the process of choosing also gives shape to those objects. The text that results is thus a representation of the author—literally, a self-portrait—as well as a description or explanation of something else.

The principle of "the disinterested search for knowledge," which as an ideal has the standing of a cliché in both scientific and humanistic learning, flatly denies this constant self-interest; the contention that a writer ought to and can detach himself from his historical context ignores the claims of both the "is" and the "ought." Grammatical means are but a small part of the matter, but it is clear that an expository writer who censors a text for personal references by the disguise of an authorial "we" or by using passive verbs which deny the author's presence as agent makes claims for the impersonality equally of writer and text; the author asks that the text be read as though it had somehow written itself. Insofar as interest in a subject is itself a significant feature of that subject, these tactics are deceptive: as they succeed, the reader is taken in by leaving the author out; if they fail, the reader has to assume a role as editor, writing the original author into his or her own text.

A premise in this continuing comparison between models of discourse is that the selection of any rhetorical instrument presupposes decisions of substance or content. Thus we understand how the ideal of an impersonal rhetoric ensures that evaluative questions will be hedged, placed in brackets—for instance, by the qualifications of indirect discourse ("It is commonly held that murder is wrong") or by excuses for editorial intrusion ("It is my own view that murder is wrong"). How could the posture of neutrality be found leaning? The thesis of the fact-value distinction that separates what is from what ought to be is implicit in the conception of the impersonal author; it is an unconscious but unmistakable irony that by this impersonality the author hopes to provide assurance that the text, in avoiding questions of value, is exactly what it ought to be. The ideal posed in such different theorists as Northrop Frye and Roman Jakobson of a literary science free from disputes about value (as implicit either in literary texts or in the theorists' own methods) means only that such issues are left for the reader to resolve for the science. The efforts in recent philosophical ethics to translate questions about value into a calculus of the ordinary language of value terms requires that the issues of what might or ought to be said in ordinary usage—and, even more, to be done—is left to the taste or impulses of individual speakers.

Harsher, and larger, than the echo of the fact-value distinction are the clash between the mechanistic metaphor borrowed by the humanities from the sciences and the questions in the humanities which that metaphor is then supposed to illuminate. Even if the assumption is fruitful in science of a reality consisting of discrete elements acting on each other from a distance, that model only subverts the characteristic issues in the humanities. The claim that human intentions and actions are consequences of prior, external causes is consistent with the ideology of physics or chemistry; but to limit the explanation of artistic form or of moral decision to the principles of efficient cause or the autonomy of individual parts is arbitrarily to rule out substantial evidence of the role of purposive design and the way in which human "entities" act. The mechanical causes which for Freud and Marx explained so much of the historical process did little, they each acknowledged, to account for the formal character of art, its "artfulness"; but this disclaimer has not restrained the influential schools of literary or historical theory that refer exclusively to psychic or economic causality for explanations of artistic or political achievement. The humanities have assumed, in these terms, that the analysis of expressive forms is identical in method to the analysis of objects that are not expressive and that can be said to have form only metaphorically. But it is far from self-evident that the analysis of a chemical "unknown" is exemplary for an artistic (or historical or moral) "unknown": we know enough about both sources to know this.

The dominance of a mechanistic model is further reflected in the evaluation which humanistic writing has come to apply to its procedures, specifically, in the principle of empirical verification. Again, the ideal here is plausible and, more notably, safe. For if propositions in a sequence of argument have been empirically isolated and tested, the conclusions that follow from the sequence will also be empirically distinct and their reference clear. But to restrict meaningfulness to such units implies that whatever is articulated *must* provide a match between propositions and equally discrete objects—that any nuance or residue on either side also falls on the other side of knowledge. This denies even the possibility that truth might be related to moral or aesthetic criteria of value, or that truth might be a function not of individual propositions but of a larger unit which is more than their sum and not discursive at all. And there is, after all, a large tradition in which truth appears as representation or symbol, as literary figure or moral realization; it is not a fault in that tradition if it fails to agree to a discontinuity between the knower and his object, or if it denies that individual and discursive propositions are the fundamental elements of representation. One has only to recall major traditions of writing outside the current ones to recognize the force of this disagreement; so, for example, the range in historiography between Herodotus and Gibbon, Tacitus and Michelet—all standing in common, independently of their differences, against an ideal of impersonality in the rhetoric of history. Philosophical counterexamples are no scarcer, in writers as remote from each other as Plato and Hegel, Descartes and Kierkegaard. Whatever their conceptions of the relation of the writer to the world written, it is hardly the relation between a reporter and a neutral or intransitive object, a reality simply waiting to be annotated.

If we ask about the harm done by writing and method in the humanities that masquerades in the costume of writing and method in the sciences, we have to compare the possible virtues of writing that does not yet exist to the defects of writing that does. But even in this phantom contrast we recognize the difference between a live person and a caricature—accentuated because the person has devised the caricature and hardly diminished by the fact that *anybody* can be caricatured. Writers, we know, are moved by interests, at least in part their own; they are speaking about themselves even when the writing by means of which they speak denies it. The ideal of detachment, neutrality, thus becomes an occasion for mystification: the bystander is invited by the writer-magician to watch him jump out of his skin. Admittedly, the allure of the prospect is understandable, both for writer and for reader: Who would not wish to see things, one's self, clearly, without affect—and then to fix a description so artless that a reader might also see through it to the thing itself? But constraints on expression, like constraints on any action, are inherent in the agent. The conceptions of the self that have turned out to be most revealing, that have come closest to realizing for human affairs the scientific ideal of disclosure, have openly—flagrantly—violated the diplomatic principles of neutrality and non-belligerance now assumed to be self-evident for rhetoric. Writers like Plato, Rousseau, Nietzsche, and Whitehead were not afraid to admit or to affirm the obvious, not even the *most* obvious: that, whatever else their writings asserted or represented, they were also, still more fundamentally, self-portraits, self-interested, self-centered. The fact that we find this same acknowledgment in the work of a few "academic" writers (like Lionel Trilling and Roland Barthes) is at least balanced by the fact that the latter figures invariably have found their places contested by academic orthodoxy.

To be sure, the question of how such claims for disclosure can oppose the larger measure of contemporary practice requires something more than only agreement that it should be done. The technology of writing in the humanities, its professionalization, reflects the professionalization of the topics written about and of almost everybody who does the writing; and the reasons for that professionalization—economic, ideological, formal—are undoubtedly larger than all of us. But the manners of writing, although they represent a collective contract and technique, are never quite beyond the manner of the individual: the majority of one may yet act—perhaps on others, but certainly on himself. The principles of action, in any event, are not difficult to recognize:

1. Do not pretend that what you write has been written outside human motive, purpose, interest. The reasons why you write, and why what you write about should be written about, are essential to the understanding (including your own) of what you write; let those reasons be part of your text.

2. Use the technical terms of an artificial language only if no other terms will do; before you use them, make clear to the reader both what they mean and why you need them. If you are surprised to find that by the time you do this you have said what you wanted to say, the surprise will soon wear off.

3. Judge in your writing as you would yourself be judged by it. Procrustes' bed, and everybody who slept on it, were allowed one size, an uncomfortable fit. Discourse, too, reflects the variations of human form; if the standards by which you shape your writing do not reflect those variations, it will tell your reader (and yourself) a good deal that no one wants to know—much of it false.

4. What you are writing about will invariably be a process, with beginnings and ends outside your control and, probably, knowledge; your writing itself joins the process. Recognize your reader (and yourself) as agents of the process. Thus: do not multiply words; do not reify verbs as nouns; use the

65

active voice rather than the passive, singular, rather than collective or mass (-ology, -ism, -ation) nouns.

5. I borrow a last principle from George Orwell's "Politics and the English Language"—a golden rule for all writing, and the more evidently so when the writer himself is also being written about: Break any of these rules sooner than say anything outright barbarous.

Orwell does not tell his reader what he means by "barbarous," but it is clear that he chooses the word to emphasize the moral (and thus potentially immoral) character of writing. Indeed, the origin of that word itself is inflammatory, intended to distinguish what is human from what is not; this—reflecting forwards and backwards as well as on the present—suggests the heat and light that the humanities would produce if they dared to write true to themselves.

8

The New Scholasticism

The Old Scholasticism was an outgrowth of the parochial church which the New Scholasticism, a product of the secular university, has been pleased to condemn. But whether one counts the number of angels who can dance on the head of a pin or the number of sibilants in a stanza of poetry, the difference does not amount to much. The genuinely important questions from which the lesser ones have broken off are obscured; the way is open in either case to the self-aggrandizement and indiscrimination that link the work of the new academy to that of its ecclesiastical forbear. And the hope that the university can matter beyond the intellectual playing fields enclosed by its walls becomes increasingly problematic as the rules of the game it is playing become more restrictive and private.

The issues from which the scholastic starts are not of themselves trivial: angels on the head of a pin can dance to the greater glory of God, and the numbering of sibilants in a line of poetry may in fact offer at least provisional entrance to the power of art. But statistical analysis is not at the point of either case; distortion sets in when the projects are mistakenly regarded as autonomous, as ends in themselves, when their origins and destinies are forgotten.

Reasons for such lapses of memory are plain enough. The logic animating the adventures of ideas is unpredictable; the odds against an effort to match illumination with issues of moment are formidable. The imminent loss of a contest in which personal stakes are high leads naturally to the refuge of the academic playing field. Articles are annotated and referred to other articles; books grow today on yesterday's corpses. The institution which sponsors the modern cleric contributes contributers to his destruction by measuring the year's productivity in terms of the number of bibliographical entries winnowed from the harvest of the brotherhood. Everybody must or does participate; and for anyone who questions the results, there are ten whose survival depends on reducing him to silence—

a contingency less (or perhaps more) ominous than it sounds, since silence can be bloodlessly enforced if only other voices speak loudly enough.

The church of the Middle Ages had a monopoly on intellect and power—and attracted because of this both the creative spirit and the sycophant who thought to make the best of an imporbable world. The university competes now in the natural sciences with the secular world of industry and business. But the produce of the humanities—here the stakes are highest and the trivial the slightest—determines by itself what the market will have to bear. Its hegemony admits to membership anyone who will live by the creed; it welcomes those who propogate the faith. Picture, if you will, the labor of the modern cloister: the sociologist-psychologist-literaturologist walking briskly and blindfolded on a treadmill which at its far end converts his energy into reprints—the minutes of interminable discussion.

Tragic as it is, the situation will not be altered by recognition of the flaw. The Old Scholasticism died only after the world that nurtured it had been distorted beyond recognition. Even before the New Science and the infusion of the Renaissance, though, the seeds of revolt—sown by its own hand—could be remarked. The doctrine of double truth won currency as a means of paying tribute to religious orthodoxy without allowing it to obscure the prospect of another—extra-religious—world. Emotional fervor, marshalled in the columns of church orders, privately subverted the ideas of that orthodoxy in mystical heresy. For those who now read the omens with the advantage of hindsight, the signs were plain.

If he could be certain that the efflorescence of a Renaissance would follow him, that his participation was a necessary condition for cultural rebirth, the contemporary cleric might attempt to defend his role as artist in the etching of historical design. The premonitions that would figure in such an apologia are compelling. Allegiance to the catechism of double truth appears now in the positivists and the statisticians who work, but do not live by that "despotism of the eye" which places fact and value in separate worlds; the mystical reaction finds support in the existentialist and anti-intellectualist polemic. The scholastic verbosity and redundance? But surely this needs to be argued least of all.

History, though, is not reliable in its dispensations. The "ism" named after Alexandria is an alternative to a Renaissance; and one might not choose to be immortalized so. Finally, of course, the decision will not be made by the academic himself. If he must submit to change, the cataclysm of the future—whatever future it is—will inform him of its terms. The prospects, as for the Schoolmen of the fourteenth century, extend beyond the grasp of academic refinement. Peace? War? One world? No world? The New Jerusalem? The New Babylon? Any alternative that resolves the current distortion offers premises which must breach the self-contemplative security of university walls and academic system. And perhaps at the end of it no one will see whether the New Scholastic goes down with his colors flying, whether in a last moment of vision he recognizes his work for what it is. Failure to do so will be the more notable, since required for that recognition is less academic sophistication than a willingness to admit the obvious. A last and ironic joke of academic history would find the scholastic disappearing into it, still unaware that it had begun.

9

The Humanities in American Life

In 1978, the Rockefeller Foundation invited thirty-two scholars, academic administrators, and representatives of foundations, the media, the arts, and business to assess the "place and prospects" of the humanities in the United States. The report of that commission was then published— intended, we learn, to serve the next decade by its analysis and thirty-one recommendations for change. The challenge to the members of any such commission, obviously, is formidable. Even if they had met in Pericleian Athens or fifteenth-century Florence, it would not have been easy for them to say exactly what it was that the humanities had accomplished there or might yet do—and as the Rockefeller Commission examined the outlook for the humanities in such settings as Bedford-Stuyvestant, St. Paul, Virginia, and the Tulsa Public Library in the 1980s, we recognize at least the qualities of courage and persistence. Still, it is the work of the report, not its intentions, that are to be judged, and on *that* count, the conclusions of the report seem finally as much a symptom of the problems which it names as a solution to them. Karl Kraus referred to psychoanalysis as the malady it was intended to cure, and something like that relation holds for the Rockefeller Report's conception of the humanities as well. This could perhaps be understood as evidence of just how deep-seated the problems of the humanities are; but it also, of course, takes something away from the conclusions reached by the commission.

The report assigns "highest priority" and its first ten recommendations for action to "the humanities in the schools" (elementary and secondary): "Our public schools are the only means for [preparing] all young men and women for participation in a democratic society"—and the humanities, the report finds, have much to do in this connection that has so far been left undone or done badly. There is a persistent tone of self-congratulation in

A response to *The Humanities in American Life,* report of the Rockefeller commission on the Humanities (Berkeley, Calif., 1980).

70

the development of this theme—as if to call attention to the daring of humanists who discuss the "lower" rather than the higher education; and although by itself this tone might be excused as only tactless, there is more serious evidence of its consequences in the commission's own history. For having at an early meeting decided to emphasize the role of the schools, the members of the commission then evidently looked around the room to discover that no one present knew much about them. About universities, institutes for advanced study, foundations, television, government—yes; but not about elementary and secondary education. The commission's reaction to this omission was to appoint as "special advisers"—*not* as members—two high school teachers and the dean of a school of education. And the moral of this small part of the story is clear: most immediately, that when humanists come to talk about the humanities, they do not expect to discuss education in the first or even in the tenth grade; but more generally, that even when the humanities as they are currently organized leave their traditional enclosures, they are reluctant to see themselves as part of the social process that has constructed those barriers—indeed, that they are reluctant to look at the social process at all. This is less a matter of elitism (although it is also that) then it is a resilient indifference to historical analysis—of themselves no less than of whatever it is they are talking about.

Such conclusions are hard to avoid even for the findings of the commission on its topic of highest priority. Nobody seriously concerned with contemporary social institutions, for example, doubts that elementary and secondary education is to a large extent a wasteland: teachers are drawn from the least able groups of college students; certification requirements for teachers are so extensive and vacuous as to make a liberal education for students who choose to be teachers virtually impossible; urban schools are the only civic institutions aside from police stations and the courts where society finds its values openly tested, and the result there, like many encounters with the law, is often a mixture of exhaustion and violence that precludes any educational ideal other than that of simply keeping the lid on. All this the commission in one form or other notices. But then we read the solutions it proposes: Recommendation 1: "Local school board members and superintendents of schools must establish the humanities as a priority in the curriculum of their distincts." Recommendation 2: "State education officials should enlist the best teachers available to help them defend the immeasurable educational value of the questions, methods, and fields of the humanities.'' Recommendation 5: ''School boards and superintendents should reduce classes to manageable size. Classes in writing should be limited to twenty students.'' Recommendation 8: ''We urge state departments of education . . . to base requirements for certification of teachers on a solid liberal education that includes the humanities.''

There is nothing wrong with these suggestions, of course; it is difficult to imagine anyone able to understand the words who would quarrel with them. But they have all the intellectual and practical bite of Canute's command to his army to whip the sea as punishment for its unruly behavior. How, we ask, do the recommendations serve the ends they are meant to accomplish?—and for *that* question, the commission takes little responsibility. It is not only that the proposals, seen as a whole, would require a very large sum of money. (The report nowhere even estimates what the cost of the thirty-one recommendations would be; nor does it offer any advice on how the likely sources of money will be persuaded to part with it. On a quick and rough reckoning, I guess that something like an additional three billion dollars [annually, non-inflated] would be required to make a substantial advance on the recommendations. This, when the total 1980 budget for the National Endowment for the Humanities, after much straining and haggling, came to 150 million dollars and when a new president, whose election the commission evidently did not consider possible, is now proposing a flat 50 percent *cut.*) The indifference to the consequences of its own recommendations is only an instance of the commission's general disregard for the historical texture of the problems it identifies in the humanities and its denial of the constraints that will affect the solutions proposed for them. Thus, it is obviously true, as the report suggests, that university-level humanists have contributed little to the shape or content of education in the secondary and elementary schools. Why *is* this? Well, surely one cause is the professionalism and specialization by which the humanists (and the university more generally) have come to measure themselves, leaving little incentive or time for reflection on social issues or indeed on *any* issues outside their own fields. Is it likely, then, that colleges and universities *will* ''encourage their faculty to help improve education in the humanities in high schools'' (Recommendation 9)? Almost certainly not—not, in any event, as long as the conditions that led to the present indifference remain unchallenged.

How to do *that* is surely a difficult problem, and we can hardly fault the Rockefeller Commission for not solving it. But the report's unwillingness to acknowledge the background to the issues for which it proposes solutions means also that it has nothing to say about the choices that will have to be made in reconstructing the humanities or about the ideological and social consequences that would follow those choices. The working principle in the report seems to be that to improve the humanities, we can simply keep what is good in them and add the features that they lack. The deficiencies found in the humanities thus appear gratuitous, matters of chance or forgetfulness—and one need not have a conspiratorial view of the past to recognize that history has never been as easygoing as *that,* that most historical choices take the forms they do because *not* everything is possible. (Even a conspiracy theorist might have been helpful to the commission, whose members were evidently chosen as if role and constituency counted for everything in theoretical or social analysis and ideology for nothing: administrators-scholars, men-women, scientists-humanists, academicians–wordly types. The status of the humanities, we infer, is a non-ideological issue—ever the message of ideology in full stride.)

The two areas on which the report focuses in addition to the role of the humanities in the schools are the "humanities in higher education" (chapter 3) and the "humanities in community and private life" (chapter 4). And again, on those topics, although the report knows *where* to find the issues, its statement of *what* they are is consistently skewed. Graduate education in the humanities, the report confirms, is in trouble: there is scanty support for students, and there are few jobs for them when they complete their degrees. The solution proposed by the report, after a plea for a national fellowship program in the humanities comparable to that in the sciences, is a reduction in the number and size of graduate programs and a revision of some of the then remaining programs to match available employment. But what, we ask, of the humanities in their standard and traditional role (which the report, after all, means finally to defend)? The possibility that academics and their administrators might persuade employers in government and business that there is no *disqualification* in historical understanding or in the abilities to read and to write clearly—

73

is not mentioned. And it is clear that if the humanities fail to make this argument, no one else will make it for them; the suggestion that the humanities might best survive by becoming something different from what they are is the sort of defense that makes enemies unnecessary. At issue here, and perhaps already too wide to bridge, is a gap like that found in England after World War I, where the balance in which humanistic learning stands is tipped by the loss of virtually a full generation, first of students and then of teachers—with no guarantee, of course, that a later generation will be able to redress the balance.

How much of a loss this would amount to depends, of course, on what the humanities are good for at best; and we might expect just such a theory of the humanities by a commission charged with examining the general prospect. The report, however, offers little direction at this level either. A quotation from an earlier speech by Charles Frankel (who until his death served as a member of the commission) cites the humanities as "that form of knowledge in which the speaker is revealed"; the report itself identifies the humanities as "a spirit or an attitude towards humanity." Not just *any* attitude or spirit, one supposes—but the likelihood of a more specific account than this soon breaks down into a definition by enumeration and calls for "sensitivity to beauty," for awareness of the "cultural heritage," for developing "verbal, perceptual, and imaginative skills." Indeed, the writers of the report *do* reveal themselves—as suspicious of theory (or at least, as reluctant to burden their readers with it). They themselves first complain about the lack of "sequence" in courses in the humanities, and then quickly exemplify that lack by failing to develop either a practical or conceptual sequence in their own thinking. So far as general values figure in the report at all, they appear as the ideals of pluralism ("a sense of what it might be like to be someone else"), tolerance ("the humanities offer clues but never a complete answer"), and the ideals of abstraction ("we learn how individuals or societies define the moral life"). These surely are values, but they are not the only ones associated with the humanities, and they are arguably not the most important ones; certainly they are not the values that most directly affect ethical action, for example, as it requires a sense of particularity more than of pluralism, a grip on practical, not on theoretical reason. But again, the distaste for questions of practice and action fits

74

closely the conception by the report of its own role: disinterested, abstract, detached from history.

This attitude, it should be clear, is more than only a mannerism or tactical choice. It has substantive consequences, and this is most evident in a significant omission in the report: among thirty-one often fulsome recommendations, not one of them even mentions the problems of discrimination by race or sex and the effects—conceptual and practical— that those deep-rooted tendencies continue to have on institutions of the humanities no less than on the society as a whole. Are we meant to infer from this silence that the commission decided that those issues, even, for example, the conception of equality, have nothing to do with the humanities? That they have nothing *in particular* to do with the humanities? It would be surprising if the commission had given way here to the natural or social sciences (the view taken of the humanities is nothing if not broad: "Like radio, newspapers are implicitly humanistic," etc.). And so the reader of the report is left to await the piety that since the humanities are concerned with humankind, they need not dignify by mention prejudices that do less than this; that the historical awareness for which the humanities are allegedly the vehicle is a *general* awareness—that is, an awareness of nothing in particular.

Notwithstanding these systematic weaknesses, the report might still be valuable for its individual prescriptions, but the few of these that seem pertinent also come largely unmotivated, appearing as intuitions or obiter dicta. It is undoubtedly true, for example, that if the "writing problem" in higher education is soluble at all, it can only be met—as the report recommends—by dispersing writing courses across the college curriculum, assigning responsibility for them to fields of the humanities other than literature and to disciplines outside the humanities as well. But when this proposal is made without any reference to the history of academic malfeasance that first conceived Freshman Comp and delivered it to the hands of English Departments—and there to the hands of a new proletariat, the TA's—not only is a fine story lost of humanistic intrigue and class warfare, but the reader is left to invent for himself exactly what the stakes are in the newly proposed change or why it would be an improvement on the past.

Finally: it may well be unfair to grade any report compiled by a committee on its writing. But a statement about the humanities that itself calls attention to the importance of language and the literary imagination might be expected to improve on the clumsy prepackaging that flavors institutional writing as much as it does institutional cooking. And once again the report is symptomatic, replete with tautologies ("If college humanists are to help prepare good school teachers, they must show genuine respect for the teaching profession") and banalities ("The Commission believes that the humanities are a social good and that their well-being is in the national interest") and weak-kneed emphasis ("While the medium in the humanities is language, the turn is toward history"). One brief moment, quite direct in mixing metaphor with desire, deserves mention even among these others: "The humanities," the report pleads, "must be a line item in institutional budgets, philanthropy, and public consciousness." The humanities may not be able to live without line items—but that does not mean, we begin to see, that survival is assured with them.

No commission on the humanities is likely to spend much of its time talking about sin (original or not). But the highmindedness and the dignified intentions of this document contrast so sharply with the profane detail and self-analysis that it should have attended to in order to make good on those intentions that probably no other starting place in experience (nonhumanistic as it may be) could have succeeded in joining the two. We wait, then, to see what the humanities—or commissions on the humanities—will have learned in the next ten years or even, on a longer view, in the decades after that.

10

Tolerance and Its Discontents
Teaching the Holocaust

Most university or college teachers would deny that the courses they teach have anything to do with ethics, let alone that they could be accused of indoctrinating students with their own values. But these teachers, too, despite themselves, wind up committing themselves on ethical issues and offering those commitments to their students. How could it be otherwise, when each time an instructor answers (or avoids) a question, something is asserted about the role of the teacher, about the ideals of education, about how students—men, women—deserve to be treated?

In this often hidden agenda, moreover, the ideal of tolerance and its corollary value of pluralism rank high. The phrase that repeats itself as a motto of higher education—the "disinterested search for knowledge"—is a formulation of just these qualities, proposing to anyone who approaches that every position or action deserves a hearing; that differences in perspective are not only likely but useful; that where evidence or argument run out, then conflicting judgments and tastes, whatever their consequences, must live together; that moral or practical reason has nothing to do with the shape of theoretical knowledge. John Stuart Mill's classic essay *On Liberty* puts the argument for tolerance not only as a civic virtue, but as an intellectual ideal: falsehood is even *necessary* for illuminating truth. It is as if truth ought for its own sake to moderate its claims, to leave nourishment for its antagonists. Nothing is ruled out, nothing is left without some claim.

Even a superficial view of political and social history since the eighteenth century shows that the struggle against authoritarianism to establish the values of tolerance and pluralism has been hard-fought—and this history often leads us to overlook the fact that the values of tolerance and pluralism in themselves exact a price. This was brought home to me recently with a severity that twenty years of university lecturing had not

77

anticipated; I had never been made to feel so sharply the difference between teaching ethics and teaching *about* ethics, between the role of the philosopher and the role of the *professor* of philosophy.

The occasion was the discussion in a small undergraduate seminar of two books about the Holocaust: Hannah Arendt's *Eichmann in Jerusalem* and Simon Wiesenthal's *The Sunflower*. Arendt moves in her much-disputed study of the "banality of evil" from a description of Eichmann's trial in 1961 to an account of the events that led up to it; Wiesenthal, in *The Sunflower*, asks a number of writers—philosophers, theologians, jurists—to judge his response to a dying SS man who asked Wiesenthal (at the time a concentration camp inmate) to forgive him for an atrocity against Jews in which the SS man had participated in a town on the Russian front. I had introduced the two books, together with other readings from history, philosophy, and literature, as a series of reflections on the nature of evil. Those sources would, I planned, offer diverse views of the central concepts of ethical (and unethical) action—as well, of course, as an outline of the concepts themselves. Anticipating the discussion of such concepts with a group of students which was itself diverse, I had felt secure at least of a common starting point: that for the texts we would be considering and the appearances in them of evil and wrongdoing, we—students and teacher, together with the authors—would share an initial recognition at least of what those *appearances* were; of what, in immediate experience, the *problem* of evil was.

But this assumption turned out to clash surely and directly with the reality of the seminar itself, and never more so than in the discussion of the two books on the Holocaust. The strongest reaction by the class to Arendt's book addressed the trial of Eichmann itself: was not that trial illegal? Were not the Israelis at fault, as wrong morally even as Eichmann, in abducting him, bringing him to trial and then executing him? The persistent reaction to Wiesenthal's book was a denial of the question it asked: 'the SS man had acted as a soldier, and since his education and training had shaped his behavior, there should be no issue either of forgiving him or of denying forgiveness. As there could be no claim for responsibility, there could also be none of guilt. In moral disputes between nations or cultures, there is no means of resolution. The SS man had done what he had done—and that was the whole of the matter so far as *moral* judgment, from this distance in time and space, could judge.'

This was not, it needs to be said, a careless or indifferent group of students that responded in this way. They were intelligent and strongly motivated, and they read carefully; they had chosen the seminar presumably because of an interest in the topic and the readings. But then, when the topic actually *appeared,* the students were—to my own first sharp reaction—simply blind to that appearance, missing its too obvious point. And the dilemma—the *moral* dilemma—forced by the students on the instructor was, in that same moment, oppressive. On the one hand, the response itself was honest: they had read the books; they had understood, from that and other reading, what had happened during the Holocaust; the questions they raised were, as questions, reasonable and earnest. They thus in a sense had earned their doubts—and this, on the principle of tolerance to which my own training and commitment had been turned meant that the issues they raised should receive serious and measured discussion, level-headed, level-toned. On the other hand stood the facts themselves, speaking—if ever facts did—for themselves: one-sided, partial, not at all tolerant. To be sure, Arendt had herself called attention to the issue of legitimacy in Eichmann's trial—but for her, too, finally, it was Eichmann and *his* actions, not the trial, that were on trial. Wiesenthal indeed asked his readers to judge his response to the SS man's request (Wiesenthal had turned away in silence, denying forgiveness). But never, by inviting judgment, does Wiesenthal doubt the *occasion* of the SS man's request. ''Look at them!! Can't you *see* what was going on there??''— this side of me wanted to yell out, to shake the well-meaning, decent, intelligent group of young men and women before me—a group that I knew to be as unlikely as any one might find to sanction such actions, let alone to repeat them.

In fact, I did shout—but not much. Mainly, I sweated, with the heat that comes less from honest labor than from having to move in two opposite directions at one time. Tolerance? Open-mindedness? Of course. Yet these did not come close to answering the occasion that was so evidently one-sided. Pleading? Cursing? Well, no doubt—but these would hardly be intelligible to the educational past of the students, the too-willing suspension of disbelief, the academic self-denial. I forced myself—quickly at the time, more slowly later—to try to understand how a reader of those books would single out the conclusions that the students had drawn. How, in considering Arendt's description of Eichmann and his history, would a reader with no disposition to favor him or anything else about the Nazis, with no inclination even to the subtle varieties of polite anti-Semitism, be led *first* to consider the legality of Eichmann's trial? How, responding to Wiesenthal's request for advice in judging the SS man, could readers object that there was no judgment to be made?

To be sure, individual students offered various reasons for reaching these conclusions. But still, the similarities in their responses disclosed a pattern that was, it seemed to me, nothing more than a reluctance to admit the possibility of moral choice or exclusion altogether, an impulse to replace the demands of ethical judgment with the deferrals of tolerance and understanding. Where, as with the instance of the SS man, there seemed no way of judging him without condemnation, exclusion, then the judgment must itself be flattened, denied: there was, we ought to conclude, neither reason nor the means. Where with Eichmann the moral enormity was more difficult to avoid, let it at least be shared with those who brought him to trial, perhaps with mankind in general. What entered these reactions could best be understood as an enlargement of the principle of tolerance: from a precept governing relations *among people* to a precept governing judgment *within the individual*. Tolerance appears first in Mill's account, for example, as a social ideal: people (others no less than oneself) have a right to self-determination, to choose the careers they want, their friends, even, finally, their own characters—however well or badly any of these turn out. But then, this ideal, intended for relations *among* people becomes internalized—as if the individual person, in the attempt to be fair, had the obligation to see *himself* as a society, as if he should renounce his own agency, declining to make judgments or discriminations on the grounds that the principle of tolerance dictates that all possible actions have equally the right to be summoned.

Precisely the opposite conclusion might, of course, be reached from this same application of the principle of tolerance: that just *because* of their freedom to act as they choose to, people then are accountable for their specific actions and the significant differences between them and their alternatives. But in order to draw this conclusion and so, later, to judge the actions for which the principle of tolerance initially provides a means—*this* requires the collaboration of another principle, in addition to that of tolerance. There must be a basis to which individual agency can look for particularity and exclusion, beyond the will to preserve alternatives. As initially the principle of tolerance sponsors a basis for generality and inclusion, so there must be a means subsequently for reaching beyond those guides, even, in a sense, of denying them. And that step, it seemed clear, was for these students alien, disfiguring.

Admittedly, when, in desperation, I asked the students to imagine themselves as Jews inside the Holocaust, their response was quick and assured: *of course* they would have acted—opposing, even attacking the machinery that threatened to destroy them. But this, too, they persisted, was not a conclusion from moral principle but instinctive, the impulse for self-defense. One could, they held, understand *why* people might resist or condemn—but this was far from claiming a reasoned justification for such responses.

This half-hearted, half-minded conclusion, it seemed clear to me, embodied the same dilemma posed more generally by the hidden agenda of the educational institution as a whole, in which our seminar was acting a small part. Not that tolerance and pluralism are not authentic values, but that *by themselves* they cannot do the work of moral judgment or action. (I leave aside here the appeal of hypocrisy, the fact that pleas for tolerance and pluralism often turn out to be only a disguise for self-serving particularity.) What tolerance and pluralism teach us is mainly how *not* to choose, how *not* to discriminate; and as important as are the moral lessons to be learned here of detachment and restraint, the renouncing of domination, they offer no basis for the positive choices that—often in the same moment—have to be made; about making *those* choices, there is no choice.

Do any such grounds for exclusion or particularity exist? Well, surely, we act and speak *as if* they did, as if less extensive communities of interests existed within the larger one, as if individual persons held certain obligations as individuals, as if the individual agent could have a basis for moral choice. And the "as if" here is all that is needed to compel acknowledgment of other principles than those of openness and tolerance, even perhaps prior to them. There has, after all, to be a "place" from which tolerance can be extended—and that place is not, either as a matter of history or as a matter of theory, arbitrarily located. It is not easy to become an individual, the master of *that* corporation. But most people manage it—some well, some badly, but nonetheless—and the choices required for this are not accidental or the result of treating all possibilities as having equal entitlements. The individual as an individual is anything but hypothetical.

I knew, as well as my students, that their reactions went well beyond their own histories, that what I chose finally to describe to them as a *possible* example of moral blindness (so the niceties of tolerance still prevailed; I would not simply *call* them blind) had its social origins; that the seminar in which I was addressing them, for which I was myself responsible, had nourished that same failing. To insulate within the walls of a classroom the willfulness and persistence of evil; to throw the Holocaust together with the worlds of King Lear, Dostoyevsky, Job, the Marquis de Sade, Plato; to talk *about* the varieties of wrongdoing as one might talk about the varieties of an art form: is this not also to assert the ideal of moral neutrality, to mock the requirements of the individual moral decision and agent? And the sides of this pedagogical dilemma, it seems to me, repeat the other, more general antinomy I have mentioned. For not only does a teacher have the professional obligation to convey to students the neutral, unvarnished forms of disinterested analysis and reflection, to carry his share of the burden of that hidden agenda; he also, in practice, has to be a source for the students of the evidence of particularity, the occasion of individual assertion, that they do not readily find elsewhere. He has in effect to provide them with *experience*—which is always, in the last analysis, one-sided, partisan, individual. Even when the facts speak for themselves, an audience has to be able to hear.

These two kinds of requirements—respect for the many, adherence to the one—are not easily met or reconciled even if the claims of each are generously acknowledged. When one of them is simply denied, then the other also becomes distorted, enlarged, dangerous. We are there, I think, with the many and the universal—reluctant, almost disabled, for the one and the particular. Teaching about a moral enormity like the Holocaust in which the facts, if ever, *do* speak for themselves, soon discloses that imbalance—that we are not now, as a culture, in much of a position to speak about moral judgment, large or small. We have the one side of it, the will to universalize; but then the specific question remains of what there is to universalize about—and surely that particular place is where moral judgment begins and ends. If it is to be made at all.

11

About the Dead, Speak
___Only ___Mainly ___Some ___No Good

Elegies have often struggled against the rhetorical conventions—if death does not give authors the freedom of an occasion, what would?—but even so, they do not usually come in unbroken blocks of 250 pages. Yet Philip Rieff's *Fellow Teachers* has all the marks of elegy, at once doleful and passionate, facing the present through the past and the past as diminished in the present. Its evocation of loss is powerful enough to command attention as it appears again more than a decade after its first publication, searching and candid enough to allow the author to include himself among the dead as well as among the mourners. That Rieff wrote *Fellow Teachers* in response to the student (and teacher) turmoil of the late '60s hardly dulls the lesson he offers to the mid '80s: dead is dead. Nothing has happened in the years between, we infer from Rieff's new preface (his "Pretext"), to suggest that the victims—the university, but that mainly as a pretext for the culture—can be more hopeful of revival now than when he first wrote. He does not even stop to consider what to make of the evidence that many more of his current readers (whether for the first or second time) have been thinking Rieff's thoughts than had thought (or would admit) them earlier. And although this omission is undoubtedly due in part to Rieff's distrust of the company he would then find himself kept by, it more certainly reflects the weight of the loss he mourns; that has not changed even if attendance at the funeral has picked up.

The irony that Rieff wrote much of *Fellow Teachers* from the non-teaching halls of All Souls' College only underscores the extent of the

---

Review of Philip Reiff. *Fellow Teachers: Of Culture and Its Second Death,* reprinted with a new preface (Chicago, 1985). What became the book *Fellow Teachers* had its origins as a "public interview" with Philip Rieff at Skidmore college in March 1971. An early version of the book was published in *Salmagundi* (Summer-Fall 1972), and the first edition of hte book was published by Harper & Row in 1973.

community he addresses and the length of the history that he now sees as past. For the "fellow teachers" he speaks to or about are not only the colleagues he hopes to interrupt as they prepare their multiple-choice exams for Soc. 101, MWF 9-9:50; *his* fellows, whose own words fall now on increasingly remote, and deaf ears, include Plato, the Rabbis of Pirke Avoth, Augustine, Thomas, Burke, Kierkegaard. If it had been difficult to keep up an end of the conversation in that company for members of a common and live institution, the possibility becomes wistful longing in a setting cut off from those founders by its own death. The university and the culture no longer teach, Rieff holds, for the sufficient reason that the authority they require in order to do it and which they once had is gone; the self-contradiction that constitutes "lower education" has won out.

Fellow Teachers, then, elegizes a culture that has been displaced by a pseudo- or, in stricter fact, a non-culture, and Rieff's address to the individual teacher reflects both this displacement—if institutions fail, *only* individuals are left—and the role of the individual teacher in sustaining culture when it *is* authentic. The idea of culture itself is thus crucial, and Rieff returns to it with elegaic repetition, elaborating on it with the powerful social understanding and wit which distinguish *Fellow Teachers* from the prolific literature of nostalgia that has become almost a standard academic genre. This understanding, to be sure, is relentlessly subversive, directed against all claims of cultural progress and against its possibility as well. On the one hand, the social sciences have offered the title of "culture" to virtually any collection of social relations, irrespective of what holds those collections together. This largesse was itself a reaction against an earlier definition—the connoisseur's appropriation of "culture" as a selective and honorific term, synonymous with "high culture." Rieff deconstructs these two accounts by subjecting one to the other. Culture for him indeed represents an accomplishment and to that extent is honorific (the contradictory is not non-culture, but barbarism). But this accomplishment does not come by "trying," and it is one that *any* group can realize.

The key here resides not in a particular set of norms or values, but in the presence of a structure within which all such standards are set. This structure is an "interdictory order" which masks the line between what is included and what is excluded, that is, which establishes the reality of prohibition. "*No* is the first word of resistance; it remains the word that needs deepest, freshest, most constant relearning . . . to articulate any culture." Without this demarcation, Rieff contends, the possibility of value itself fails: there is no authority, internal or external—and thus also no memory and no history, nothing from which the individual mind which gives culture its content (as well, we suppose, as its discontents) can learn or establish an identity. Culture originates and sustains itself, in other words, only in the space created by repression and denial. And if we hear in this definition echoes of the cultural pessimism of the master-teacher Freud—it is Freud, not Rieff who would write that "Every individual is virtually an enemy of culture"—and even something of T. S. Eliot's tendentious "Definition of Culture," we also find in Rieff's litany of cultural loss a specific portrait of cultural character which family resemblances alone do not account for. Thus, although one side of Rieff's book points toward a general theory of culture, elaborating with rich detail the point we find stated more sparely in Mary Douglas's epigram—"Where there is dirt, there is system"—the other is addressed to a specific historical passage: his own and that of his fellows.

It is not difficult to understand, in any event, why in basing his description of the latter on this conception of the requirements for culture, Rieff finds mainly desolation around him in the present. For modern science and technology, nothing is in principle impossible, not even changes in the so-called laws of nature (by the very fact that they can be called "so-called") which themselves, after all, have served as secular versions of prohibition. The sacred orders of church and of country have, of course, been disrupted; authority—where any vestige remains at all—has been displaced by power. The university, too, emblematic of the whole because it combines a sacred order with powerlessness (surely here Rieff exaggerates needlessly), is under siege by "privileged vandalism." The effect of this vandalism has been a systematic transgression of values by many of his "fellow teachers" who have consented to the substitution of experience for knowledge, change and originality for continuity, therapy for teaching, the promise of universality in place of a "science and art of limits." Where everything is possible and immediate, there can be neither learning nor teaching—nor, as a condition for those, culture itself. Yeats, when he announced that the center no longer held, did not know the half of it: there are many centers, and they *all* hold, equally and only too well.

It would require repression on a large scale to ignore or to deny the evidence on which Rieff bases this anatomy of disorder. The irony that a society with more access to more information than any society before it should also suffer from the loss of cultural memory seems itself to be part of the will—"dead ironies" here joining "dead metaphors"—that moves the institutions which Rieff attacks. It is in any event the emphasis on the blind equality of information, the absence of discrimination among its kinds or final causes, that is in good measure the object of his criticism. The "radical contemporaneity" that has traveled as an ideal of science to the liberal arts and the university generally extends also to the society as a whole—in the language it uses, in the arts it enjoys, in its politics. The loss of history and the challenge to authority, moreover, are not incidental casualties of modernism; they are, Rieff claims, intrinsic to its design.

To be sure, an alternate view of the same evidence could find in it a *defense* of contemporary culture, but Rieff barely acknowledges this possibility (here again, the elegy in all its one-sidedness). It might be objected, for example, that the lost social interdictions of the past were not only repressive but inequitably and arbitrarily so; as against *this* price, the argument might conclude, Rieff should hardly cavil at the price to be paid for liberation. But this objection, Rieff would claim, confuses the issues: it is not the *price* of the therapeutic society that he objects to, but what one gets after paying it. There is no point in comparing costs if, with one of them, the culture itself is sacrificed.

This conclusion may seem part of a circular argument: culture requires repression or interdiction because without these there is no culture. But the circle is broken for Rieff by the history he elegizes. For if Western culture indeed had the form he claims, then, even if one dissents from his characterization of the *present,* his view of the conditions required for culture has at least the past on its side—the dead proving useful one last time. Even the issue of whether the past he recalls ever *really* existed, however, is limited in its consequences. It is not only that elegies are intrinsically partial, but that the aspect of culture which Rieff singles out as essential—the role of prohibitions—seems undeniable in that past. All that remains to quarrel about, in fact, is the proportion or balance of his judgment—not whether an interdictory order once existed, but what else, perhaps inevitably, accompanied it.

In considering this question, Rieff himself is too stern a witness even as elegist to speak only good of the dead (more of this below); and since it is also a premise of conservative epistemology that we do not have to know all the facts in order to know some of them (this constraint is itself a prohibition denied in the therapeutic society), to object to his view of culture on historical grounds is to quarrel with something more than the historical claims alone. Finally, in fact, if we bracket Rieff's historical account, we face the question of the present and the future—what, in other words, is to be *done?* And here Rieff's role as elegist wavers, not in its logic but because he has little comfort to offer beyond memory itself. The moments when Rieff allows himself to extract hope from the past so as to improve the present or lay the ground for a future, are marked invariably by breaks in his elegaic tone; like a mourner who when he hears footsteps, looks up, hoping against reason to see the dead person enter the room once again, Rieff's sense of reality is itself in the past, not in the present.

This does not mean that the proposals he makes are not consistent with his view of culture; it is just this consistency in fact which blocks his view of the present. So, for example, death is the most obvious of all interdictory limits; it is consistent then that the "practical" suggestions Rieff makes should focus on the role that death itself might have, whether in its natural or its social appearances. Thus the efforts of our therapeutic society to escape that natural interdiction either by the "taking of life" in the abortion clinic or by the re-creation of life in the laboratory should themselves be rejected (prohibited?). This does not mean, on the other hand, that death may not also serve as a social instrument. Indeed, if the awareness of limits is prerequisite for culture, then guilt as the obverse side of repression is also a cultural necessity—and punishment is an obvious means of "generating" guilt. So the place of capital punishment as social (and public) ritual ought to be restored—not for its deterrent effect (which it may not have) against particular crimes, but in order to confirm the social ideal of limits, that is, as a *general* deterrent.

The few other practical suggestions that Rieff makes seem hardly more likely to have the effects he would wish for. The "destruction of the family'' is one cause (or is it symptom? always *that* question) of the failure of authority—but the reader is left to ask for himself whether in order to repair this Rieff would require prohibitions against divorce or deny equality to the sexes. (Such possibilities are judiciously balanced in Rieff's account by his objection to efforts in the church to dilute the requirements of priestly celibacy.) To be sure, the institutions of education offer larger targets: courses in driver education could have no place where the curriculum properly consisted of ''readings, writings, and arithmetics.'' Rieff does not name the texts of his revised curriculum, but it is not difficult to infer that here, too, the authority both in and of the past would rule. And although there are large differences in understanding— and authority—between Rieff and the purveyors of ''cultural literacy'' in the Reagan Department of Education, only his general doubts about the future seem to bar the comparison at this point.

Rieff himself provides the surest explanation of why all such proposals must in the end seem lame and helpless: ''The negative gifts [of an interdictory order] cannot allow themselves to be taught.'' This is in part for Rieff another echo of the Freudian background: ''If we are aware of our repressions, then we are not repressed,'' he stipulates, adding weight to the condition that culture cannot be willed. (So an echo also of Eliot's statement that ''culture is the one thing we cannot deliberately aim at.'') If revival is possible, then, it must come through individual figures— teachers—who convey authority and the sense of limits *in* their teaching, not by precept or by the design to create a culture. But how such teachers are to announce or establish themselves in a non-culture, overcoming the resistance of a society whose genius is spent, as Marcuse had described it, in *preventing* reflection, remains unstated. Here finally, the paradox familiar from almost every important work of cultural nostalgia confronts Rieff's address to his fellow teachers as well; we recall Plato's wistful response to the question of when we could expect to see his Republic in the flesh: ''Until philosophers be kings or kings philosophers. . . .'' The prerequisite of culture seems to be culture itself.

Rieff is unwilling, moreover, to privilege himself in this prospect with any power other than that of memory and recognition. He would write *Fellow Teachers,* but he is not himself an ''apostle.'' ''Don't count on me,'' he admonishes—and here, too, we see the important line between elegy and prophecy that marks out the ironic divide of Rieff's elegy. The prophet may also lament ironically (so, for example, Jeremiah: "You have not listened to me in proclaiming liberty every one to his brother . . . behold, I proclaim a liberty for you, saith the Lord, to the sword, to the pestilence, and to the famine . . ."), but he would hardly deny or even question the future. The enormity of his task or the possibility of failure would never be concerns for the prophet—but these indeed are what cause Rieff to look backwards constantly and as a matter of principle.

Rieff's hesitation about the future, moreover, reflects doubts even about the past that he elegizes. For viewed in their historical detail rather than for their general aura, the interdictions which governed the past were often accompanied by severe consequences. If, for example, the price of culture were to require a return to the "dead" church civilization which remains a central character in any dramatization of the Western past, Rieff declines the offer: "I am a Jew. No Jew in his right mind can long for some variant of that civilization." It is not clear if Rieff is willing to offer a similar dispensation for Christians, but quite aside from this, his willingness to speak ill in addition to good about the dead strains two central links in his conception of culture: the contention that repression must be unconscious to be culturally effective, and the claim that culture is intrinsically partial or tendentious. On the first of these, it is difficult to see how *any* appearance of a true culture could be judged adversely, even by those who suffer from it (they, too, after all, would have the benefits of living in a "sacred order"). On the other hand, if "a universal culture is a contradiction in terms," as Rieff maintains in his continuing war against Enlightenment ideology, the partiality that then becomes endemic to culture can hardly avoid privileging one group over (or against) another. (If repression and interdiction are indeed keys to culture, Rieff seems to let the opportunity slip by of considering what happens to a group which by being the *object* of repression makes culture possible.)

The most notable absence from Rieff's account, the more evident because of his "profession" of sociology, is a role for social cause: what, acting with or on the individual consciousness, has produced the death of culture that he mourns? Once again, there is consistency here: if the sin of a therapeutic and technological culture is to dissolve limits, and, by denying a role to the self, to absolve responsibility, then the failure of culture, like its one-time success, must be due to individuals. But this conclusion seems quite implausible; to see the individual consciousness or will as entirely self-motivated requires so partial a view of history that his reader might here suspect that even Rieff's qualified piety has left the dead looking a good deal larger than life. Is barbarism *only* an act of will? Do industrialization, the development of technology and science, the massive increase of world population, even plain "moral luck" (often bad) have *nothing* to do with the fate of culture (the actual one or the ones that might have been)?

It could be argued that Rieff ignores such considerations because he is concerned only with those factors that *are* open to influence. But Rieff anticipates and rejects this possibility. The most immediate consequence of admitting a role for social cause in the history of culture would be to politicize the role of the teacher—and since "our first aim as teachers is . . . to depoliticize our teachings . . . to reteach ourselves unpolitical recognitions of that sacred order which is always and everywhere in authority," *any* claim for politics will be too much. This conclusion seems in fact to provide a means of understanding what has gone wrong with both politics and culture—since democracy, if it is not the inevitable end of politics as such, has certainly been the end of the politics we know and also, in Rieff's terms, the end of anything like an interdictory order. The "betrayal of the clerics" which Benda announced on much slighter evidence, has become a full-scale betrayal of the mind and the culture. It is not clear whether the political order which would thus, on Rieff's recommendation, be left to itself, could be self-sustaining in the same way that the sacred order of culture has been. If it is not (as seems likely), then a large question remains of who, if the teachers are not to be engaged, will care for the politics. Rieff here seems so concerned with the purity of culture that he would willingly doom the political life within which it is inevitably set. The fact that for the classical and even the biblical traditions of the West, the life of the individual is assumed to be tied to the existence—and the *idea*—of the community, evidently represents for Rieff either an entirely different kind of politicalization or one which excess has transformed into something quite different. Either way, his conclusion remains the same: the politics and the politicians will be untaught—and who, it might be asked, needs teaching more?

Rieff writes elegiacally because in the presence of death we first look backward, to the past, with the shadow of death cast forward to the future as well. Even such deliberate reflection on the past, however, is partial, meant to offer the survivors what consolation the present can support, with memory serving as a buffer for the present and as an anticipation of the future. This sense of historical continuity, even when it depends on a mythic selectivity from the past, is undoubtedly an important, probably a necessary condition of culture in *any* sense, honorific or not. And if, as history attests and as Rieff also—against himself—concurs, it is not by individual decisions that an interdictory order can be installed, perhaps there is no more than his fellow teachers conscientiously can do now than to join with Rieff in commemorating the past, with the hope that this act itself may somehow admit them to that history. But to stop here is also to deny the possibility of a commitment that, however illusory in design, may be necessary even to the act of remembrance and is certainly required if remembrance is ever to have a place in a live present. Rieff would probably reject such illusions even if, with them, cultural revival were possible: elegies, too, become farce if history—or culture—repeats itself. Yet also for mourners to whom the death mourned is most real, there is a life after death—namely, their own. And the question of what life that will be continues to confront them no matter how passionate and ennobling an elegy the dead they recall have inspired. Thoreau asked, "Are we not always living the life that we imagine we are?" With Rieff doing our imagining, we are already "living" inside the tomb—a strange and contradictory sensation, even when the occasion has been imagined for us by a remarkable fellow teacher.

12

Normal Academic Progress

Self-flagellation is an art of the possible, one that academics are better at than politics. Like the writer Borges, who informs his critics that he could easily supply them with harsher things to say about him than any they were likely to discover for themselves, the profess-ors (faculty, students) of higher education seem absorbed, almost inspired by their failings. Admittedly, part of the incentive for this scrutiny comes from outside: peevish legislatures, a slumped economy, the scarcity of students because of a birth rate that, cunningly, falls as the level of education rises—that is, as the universities succeed. But even together, such pressures do not account for the sense of dissatisfaction which is evident on university campuses today and of which the ideology of job seeking—pre-professional training for students and alternate careers for faculty—is a revealing symptom, but only one of many.

This malaise in the academy is neither surprising nor underserved. Some of it, surely, has been well earned by that combination of historical forgetfulness and scrambling professionalism which accompanied the rejection by the university of its traditional role as transmitter and apologist for the culture and which have offered in its stead only the standard figures of worldly success or failure. Where there is no community of purpose, no acknowledgment of the probability of history—neither future nor past— the result, predictably, will be the one we have: a thin and restless present where the pursuit of knowledge becomes only another competitive sport.

But however harsh and punitive, these qualities do not appear alone. A second side of the academic character is less dramatic but needs also to be recognized; that side is represented by the significant advances at the university in what might have been, in what *should* have been but clearly were not, certain elementary principles of institutional and social justice. The most effective display of these principles is evident in the current membership of the university, in the fact that a clear majority of that membership—women, blacks, Jews, Catholics—would quite simply not have *been* there fifty years ago. Not very much present as undergraduates, still less as graduate students, very little as faculty, hardly at all as administrators. It is only too easy, moreover, to guess what these different groups of people would have been doing instead.

Admittedly, the change involved here has been due in part to causes that have nothing to do with moral principle; no one could claim, furthermore, that the change has been universally accepted, let alone welcomed, or that it has been consistently applied. Decisions and verdicts still pass through the agency of individuals where there can be no insurance against prejudice or stupidity or the combination they often make. But the emergence of the principles is unmistakable, nonetheless, stipulating a system of due process and rights that had long been denied in the university—as they were and even now continue to be denied in the other professions and in the world of business on which, as Thorstein Veblen pointed out, the American university had been modeled. Not only the principles themselves but a conception of the university are at issue here. The changes in the former imply that the university is no longer entitled to claim the medieval "benefit of clergy" (literally or metaphorically)—that device by which the university attempted to maintain itself as an island, answering to its own laws and judges and thus effectively conserving its *own* past even more than that of the culture. It admitted or excluded as it chose to; decisions within its circle were thus also compounded of will and intuition rather than law or due process.

The difference made by the loss of this sense of privilege may be seen in several examples drawn from the past, each about a distinguished American academic figure. The first of these concerned Lionel Trilling's appointment to a position in the English Department at Columbia University; the second, a series of incidents in the history of the Department of Philosophy at Harvard, recounted by Bruce Kuklick in his *The Rise of American Philosophy*. The former is, to be sure, only one of many episodes in the history of anti-Semitism in the American univeristy, dramatic mainly because the figures involved were Trilling and Columbia. Trilling himself, we know, came perilously close to being denied an appointment there. But the true punchline came only after that struggle had been successfully concluded (it is retold in Alfred Kazin's *New York Jew*). Then the chairman of the English Department felt obliged to console Clifton Fadiman, also Jewish, also a new Ph.D., who had at the time also hoped for an appointment: "We have room for only one Jew," the chairman reported to Fadiman, "and we have chosen Mr. Trilling."

There are any number of such stories to be told about quotas, about religious and racial exclusion from teaching and studying in the university which was at the same time professing its own "disinterested" commitment to knowledge. The practices were explicit and virtually unashamed; there was no recourse for the victims inside or outside the university, and there was little pressure from either side even for concealing the practices, let alone for changing them. If they were not regarded as just, they were at least viewed as not unjust.

The same casualness with respect to moral principle and precedural safeguard is evident in an earlier series of incidents retold in Kuklick's book; I mention three of them. The first of these involved Charles Sanders Peirce, recognized since as the most original philosopher America has produced, but who, even if he had been less than that, would hardly have earned the verdict passed on him by the academy. After working on the fringes of university life for fifteen years following his graduation from Harvard in 1863, Peirce was hired as a lecturer at John Hopkins on a series of annual appointments. During that time, he had been led to expect a permanent appointment—but suddenly, in the middle of his fifth year, he was dismissed by the president, Daniel Coit Gilman. Gilman did not state the reasons for his action, and they are still not known precisely; but the evidence is strong that the circumstances of Peirce's divorce and remarriage within a period of several months (in 1883) were the main factors. Nothing else that was both known and new in Peirce's life occurred at the time, and certainly this was the cause as his contemporaries understood the dismissal. Even those who regretted the latter, however— William James, for example—did not think to contest either it or Peirce's subsequent blacklisting; in the years till his death in 1914, Peirce was never again to hold an academic post. In 1892, when James recommended Peirce to the University of Chicago for a position there, G. H. Palmer, then chairman of the department at Harvard, wrote negatively to President Harper at Chicago, impugning James's recommendation on the grounds of Peirce's "broken and dissolute character."

The second episode occurred in connection with a request submitted to President Eliot in 1894 by Mary Calkins, later an important psychologist, that she be granted a doctorate in philosophy. Women were not then permitted to register at Harvard as graduate students, but Calkins had attended the required classes in philosophy and had completed the work in them as well as the other requirements for the degree. Hugo Musterberg endorsed her request with a statement to President Eliot that Calkins was then his best pupil. "The Corporation," Eliot responded, "are not prepared to give any Harvard degree to any woman no matter how exceptional the circumstances may be."

The third item concerns the prospective appointment of A. O. Lovejoy to the Harvard faculty at a time (1914–1917) when the Department of Philosophy was attempting to recoup the loss of the principal figures of its "Golden Age": James, Santayana, and Royce—and when Lovejoy, it was agreed by the members of the department, was preeminent among the likely candidates. President Lowell twice vetoed this nomination, each time for the same reason: Lovejoy had been active in founding the American Association of University Professors. He was, in Lowell's phrase, a "trouble-maker."

Now, as moral wrongs go, such statements or actions hardly deserve the attention that other wrongs would; they do not involve murder or torture, and even the specific damage they caused can only be speculated about. But they nonetheless effectively introduce the concept of moral blindness; in them, too, we are left with the question of how the agents responsible for them *could* have spoken or acted as they did. Did they know what they were doing—these leaders of the dominant institutions of learning and civility in the culture—and do it anyway? Was it in them only a failure to see the possibility that accomplishment might be judged apart from the person? Was it a concept of the person that they lacked? How—we learn as a question from these other questions—does *anyone* fall victim to or acquiesce in or escape from moral blindness?

Admittedly, few questions of this kind, asked as they are in the abstract, admit to ready answers. The history of ethics, as philosophers and moral teachers have conceived it, simply assumes the moral point of view and provides little understanding of its alternative and not much more of its failures. If this were not the case, the biblical and the Greek visions of the good, compelling as they were, could hardly have found a place so readily for the practice of slavery. The means of advance here, it seems, can only be, first, by recognition of the incongruity and then by an enlargement of the moral order to include and so to neutralize the incongruity: slaves, it turned out, could be seen first as persons.

This is, it seems to me, the kind of advance evident now in the university, one which will not always prevent incidents such as those I have referred to, but which, as they occur, insures that they can be called to account by principles of social justice and due process. Hiring and firing by presidential fiat, exclusion on the grounds of religion or gender, the punishment of personal idiosyncracy—these could not pass now as entitlements of membership in the university. There is now at any university deserving of the title a forum in which the issues are at least heard; there will be judges, within the university as well as outside it, aware that principles *are* at issue in them.

Undoubtedly, some university presidents and faculty and even students remain committed to the model of the university as a center of natural privilege and thus as entitled to claim the benefit of clergy in its own procedures—and *thus,* from the top down, sanctioned in making decisions on the basis of personal will and preference. Moreover, there are obviously ways in which even without openly professing it, administrations and faculty can still put this sentiment to work. But language is not without power, we know—and so is silence; the fact that few university administrators or faculty would dare publicly to say the words recited in the incidents I have referred to is itself a power against them. As in so many of its appearances, justice comes here in the restraints it imposes, the wrongs it may avert rather than the positive good it commands. It is in these terms, too, that we can understand the difference between due process and the quotas or "goals" designed as temporary measures to redress a social wrong, on the one hand, and the practice of arbitrary exclusion which first constituted the wrong, on the other.

It may be objected that the evolution of the university as I have been pointing to it comes at the cost of the university's traditional and more valuable role as a source of "disinterested" knowledge and, more than this, as an agent—the principal agent—of historical continuity and transmission in the culture. These are inevitably lost, the claim goes, as the institution politicizes itself, views itself as giving up its insulated position and as taking sides on the social and legal issues affecting the context in which it is set. But the losses on both these counts are, I believe, fictions—and to see this, one has only to look to the actual accomplishments of the "higher" learning in the nineteenth and the early twentieth century. It may be that with Mark Hopkins at one end of a log, a student who could keep his balance at the other end would have been well educated—but it would not have been just any student who could have held his place there, as Mark Hopkins was not just any teacher. Such evidence as there is of student accomplishments and competence fifty years ago—college records and catalogues, memoirs, even the history of their later careers—reveals less rather than more in the way of achievement in comparison to students of the 1980's, and this is still more clearly the case for the faculty. There is much to be said against the recent professionalization of research and teaching which has been a consequence of opening up the university; but it would require an unabashedly partial eye to prefer to it the schoolmasterish sense of privileged leisure that dominated teaching at the American university in the nineteenth and early twentieth centuries. And this only makes the comparison even up, without taking into account the ideal of general—"mass"—education which has absorbed much of the energy of higher education in the last fifty years and which still, to its honor, distinguishes American higher education from programs of education in other countries.

To the argument that social justice is not properly the business of the university, the answer can only be that the university could not avoid taking a position on that ideal even if it chose to. It might, of course—and in the past often did this—simply accept the conventions of the society around it. But acceptance is also affirmation; that such a response may come with reservations of conscience or in a spirit of political neutrality does not diminish the force of the acceptance itself. Admittedly, the instruments of the new sense of justice have sometimes proved dull or cumbersome; they have brought with them bureaucracy, litigiousness, the inflated rhetoric of some "affirmative action" programs, even new injustices. But these costs of the cure are still slight when measured against the harm of the social diseases to which they have been applied. The pretense of moral neutrality is more dangerous even than moral neutrality itself, and the university seems now to have acknowledged the menace in both. Not enthusiastically, perhaps, not consistently, not brilliantly—but nonetheless. Normal academic progress, in other words.

III Politics at More Than Its Word

13

Politics and the Death of Language
Orwell's Newspeak

Orwell's use of "1984" for the title of his book was not exactly an accident, but neither was it entirely a matter of choice: he arrived at it, we know, by transposing the last numbers of "1948," the year in which he completed work on the book—and he did this only after his publisher had objected to his original title that referred, more pessimistically, to *The Last Man in Europe*. The year 1984 itself, then, had no special significance for Orwell. It was meant to stand for some date in the future—in the not-too-distant future—when a combination of forces familiar to him from events in the then recent World War II might come together to form the brutal, efficient, and totalitarian society that Orwell depicts in his novel. In that society, the individual person is, for all practical purposes, abolished—a possibility, Orwell insists, which is a modern "accomplishment." For there are significant differences, he claims, between even the harshest governments of the past and modern totalitarianism—not so much in what the former *wanted* to do, but in what they could do. Undoubtedly the older despotisms would have chosen to be totalitarian if they were able to; but they lacked the necessary means, the sheer efficiency and the related sense of purpose required for the full control by a government of anything said or written or even thought by its citizens that characterizes totalitarianism. As these requirements become reality, there is nothing left to the individual person except a body—and that, of course, is even more easily dominated. It is just this ideal of control that Orwell identified with totalitarianism and which, as it takes over, makes Winston Smith, Orwell's main character in *1984* and the closest thing to a hero there until he too gives up the fight, the "last man in Europe."

Did Orwell believe that the kind of world he describes in *1984* was inevitable? That given the developments of recent history, there is no way to prevent totalitarianism from taking over? Any such claim seems too strong. It is clear that Orwell was not very optimistic, from his view of human nature, of how people were likely to treat each other; yet in all his writing, the values of decency and truth are so strongly represented, even when they are eventually defeated (as they are in *1984* or in *Animal Farm*), that readers might well conclude that those values *could* have won—or more to the point, that they may yet win. For himself, moreover, Orwell felt that by writing *1984,* by making his readers aware of what the future *might* hold for them, he could perhaps help to prevent it from happening. There was, in short, the possibility of escape.

On the other hand, the forces working to produce 1984 are powerful indeed, and much of this power comes from the fact, as Orwell saw it, that they are in some measure quite beyond the control of individual persons. Orwell had been sufficiently influenced by Marxist thinking to believe that what happened in history was affected to a great extent by social forces larger than the actions or even the lives of individual people. And if that were true, then, if the political system portrayed in *1984* did come into existence, this would not occur because people at the time were somehow worse, morally or intellectually, than those who had lived earlier. Orwell held the view, in fact, that people across the ages of history were by and large pretty much alike, with villains and saints fairly well distributed and with a bit of each of those present in almost everybody. (He distrusted the saints—Gandhi, for example—as much as he opposed the villains.)

So it is not just the actions or even the failings of individual people that account for significant changes in history. And if we ask, then, what could produce the totalitarian society that Orwell describes in *1984,* where the lives of individuals were externally controlled in every activity that mattered, where history and truth were held to be what the political rulers decided that they were, we need more than the simple explanations that all power corrupts, or that the citizens of a society get the government that they deserve, true as these judgments may be in their own ways. This does not mean that we can know in advance what conditions would lead to totalitarianism in a country, for example, that had had a liberal and democratic tradition (the country described in *1984* is pretty clearly a latter-day version of the England in which Orwell was writing), much less that any *single* cause is likely to produce such a change. But surely, among the factors that could turn Orwell's *1984* into reality, the development of technology and the mechanization of society—and with these, the growing presence of what might be called technological thinking—are likely candidates; it is clear, in any event, that Orwell himself had this general factor very much in mind as he tried to imagine in 1948 what life would be like in the future.

Consider, for example, two related features of social organization that are present in Orwell's *1984* and that are also implicit goals of *any* totalitarian government: first, the ability of a central authority to know at every moment, accurately and in detail, what the citizens of the society are doing and saying (and so, also, what they are thinking); and second, the ability of that central authority to control the information or knowledge available to the people under the authority. Both these conditions are presupposed if full control is to be established over individual lives: since people are to know or to think only what they are supposed to, there must be a way of monitoring what they *do* know and think. To achieve such control in a complex society required just the kind of sophisticated technological apparatus that Orwell anticipated in his novel: instant communication across long distances; the capacity for long-distance eavesdropping and spying; a central and computerized store of information that can regulate—and then, change at will—the information available to members of the public.

Speed itself is crucial here: it would be a hindrance if people with conflicting information or ideas should speak to each other, since then they would begin to wonder about the differences between their stories. They might even begin to imagine that they had *individual* memories or other powers of mind independent of the central authority—and this, of course, would be at odds with what they were supposed to believe: memory, too, was to be determined by the state. And there must also be a single meeting point for all the varieties and sources of information, a common and simplified language into which they can all be translated. The technology needed to accomplish these ends was far enough advanced even when Orwell wrote *1984* to permit him to assume that in principle they could eventually be *fully* realized—and developments in the forty years since only reinforce this belief: they are certainly possible. Without such technological advances—for example, with a network of human spies instead of electronic surveillance—political structures might still be despotic and barbarous (and, of course, there have been such societies which had no great dependence on technology); but they would lack the impersonal-character and sense of domination that mark the forms of social existence in Orwell's *1984*.

These are only examples of the technological devices presupposed in the world that Orwell describes; many others are mentioned in his work (for instance, the control of emotions by drugs). And it should not be much of a comfort, Orwell insists, to be told as we frequently are when we consider the consequences of these so-called advances, that technological discoveries or inventions are morally neutral, that they can be used for good as well as for evil, and that the decisions which determine how technology will be used are entirely up to the people who have access to it. Together with a number of later and more systematic writers on technology (for example, the French author, Jacques Ellul and the American Herbert Marcuse), Orwell was aware that the most dangerous potential of technology may finally be less in the *specific* machines or implements it produces than in the way of thinking, of absorbing and interpreting experience, that has accompanied the technological revolution and seems to be fostered by it. With its emphasis on the human control of nature and on "problem solving," technology easily leads both its producers and its consumers to view experience as such in just these mechanical terms, objectifying questions of value into factual questions of what will work or not, turning people as well as things or events into "problems" that are then to be solved or dealt with. Technology, in other words, does not simply involve the construction of new machines or instruments or techniques that may then, neutrally, be put to uses that are decided on independently: the very process of their construction, of *thinking* technologically, may affect those who do it more broadly and deeply than does the particular problem that is being addressed. We see how this influence works quite clearly in the characters portrayed by Orwell in *1984* who not only make use of the technological devices described there, but who are themselves altered in their thinking and in their characters at least in part by that association.

As I have suggested, none of these dangers implies that technology, or any other single or even combination of causes, leads inevitably to *1984*.

On the other hand, it is important to recognize that the society that Orwell projected into the future does not have to come true in *all* its details in order to be real in some of them—and we can hardly avoid recognizing that certain aspects of what Orwell predicted has already become actual: whatever else may be said about *1984,* it is no mere fantasy. We know this in a number of ways that already affect practical details in everyday life (for example, in the centralized stores of information that exist about every one of us), and we know it even more surely from certain large-scale events of recent history. Probably the two most extraordinary and consequential phenomena to have occurred in the twentiety century—in addition to the discovery of totalitarianism itself—are the "invention" of genocide (as in the Nazi attempt to exterminate the Jews) and the contrivance of the possibility of "omnicide"—the destruction of human life and perhaps of all life as a consequence of nuclear war. It is no accident that these "discoveries" occur when they do: each is closely tied to the technological advances that are a mark of the same period. Neither of them could have become possible without a number of quite specific technological inventions, some of them anticipated by Orwell, some even more ingenious than those he imagined; neither of them would have been possible without a way of thinking and organizing experience that turns supposedly advanced and "rational" societies into instruments of technology—and that changes people, even when they think they are making their own decisions and living their own lives into instruments whose actions are directed by other agents.

This has been, so far, a general description of how Orwell imagined the prospect of political totalitarianism and its relation to technology. And one might ask, what, if anything, those political and social issues have to do with language, let alone with the "death of language" mentioned in my title. A number of steps need to be considered individually which make this connection clear; these steps culminate in the language of "Newspeak," the version or dialect that passed for standard English in Orwell's *1984* and that is closely tied to the other social changes that would also have taken place by then. As Winston Smith was to be for Orwell the last man in Europe—the last person who thought or felt or cared as a human being—so Newspeak marks for Orwell the end of language and its replacement by a mechanical, depersonalized means of communication, useful mainly as a political instrument, and, at that, as an instrument of repression. Man and language, in other words, die together—and this is no accident, since for Orwell, language was not only a useful tool, but even before that, a direct expression or reflection of human character and values. Like people, language too could be honest, sincere, courageous; and so also, it could be deceitful, hypocritical, corrupt—not only when it was explicitly telling lies (which in a way, after all, is still a form of truth), but even more so as lies can be built into the fabric of the language itself, into vocabulary, into expression, even into grammar. This is just what happens to language—partly as cause, partly as effect—in the society of *1984*.

It may be helpful to recall that Orwell was concerned with the question of the relation between language and society long before he wrote *1984*: that relation, in fact, was not far from his mind in anything he wrote. Some of this attentiveness on Orwell's part comes from his continuing interest in the act of writing itself. There is hardly a literary form—with the exception, I believe, of drama—that Orwell did not experiment with. At least a couple of his early novels—which are more traditional in their plots and characters than *1984* is—are still worth reading on their own and aside from the fact that Orwell was their author. He wrote poetry (mainly for himself); when he worked for the BBC during the war, he wrote radio scripts; *Animal Farm,* which ranks with *1984* among his most popular writings, is a combination of allegory and fable; his long essays report autobiographically on events drawn from his own experience—when he walked with the hoboes around the English countryside (he writes about this in *Down and Out in Paris and London*) or when he fought (and was severely wounded) in the Spanish Civil War, events that he describes in *Homage to Catalonia*. In these, he combines historical writing with a strong fictional impulse—and the same combination appears in his shorter essays which, simply as examples of writing, are often judged to be Orwell's most original and valuable work. He was, in short, a writer rather than a novelist, and a writer with a strong social conscience; it should hardly be surprising, then, that a constant theme in his thinking and writing concerned the role of the writer in society, and the way in which what happened in a society, in the changes of its social or political

or economical structures, affected the writer's principal means of work—
that is, the language available for his use.

One premise in Orwell's conception of language, then, is just this: that
language, the words we employ in speaking and writing and the way we
put them together, reflect what is going on—and also, by implication,
what is *not* going on—in the politics and culture of the society more
generally. Language is thus a mirror of society and of history, displaying
in its own organization the events and relations that otherwise affect more
openly the lives of its users. Now in some ways, of course, this premise
will seem obvious and not especially interesting. We are aware, for example, that new words are constantly entering the language—for instance,
in names for new inventions, like "robots" or "lasers"—and most of us
also know that old words often change their meanings over time, with
certain meanings or words dropping out of the language altogether. So,
for instance, to choose one of many possible examples, the word "sophisticated" which I used earlier to refer to the more complex and advanced—
sophisticated—instruments that technology has recently produced, was
applied in the nineteenth century to things that had been *falsified* or *adul-
terated,* mixed with a strange substance; the term suggested a step backwards rather than progress; it was not a compliment at all.

Again, many shifts in usage similar to this could be cited, and we take
the fact that such changes are going on all the time pretty much for
granted. Indeed, we take it so much for granted that we do not often look
for explanations of why the changes occur, either in individual words or
for the general shifts in linguistic style that most interested Orwell. It was
in the network or pattern of relations among the individual parts of language that Orwell believed the relation between society and language most
clearly showed itself. *How* something is said or written is, for Orwell,
closely related to *what* is being said—the one *affects* the other; and since
this is as true in the life of a society as it is in the life of an individual,
then the language of a culture as a whole, its literature and its speaking,
will in effect be portraits of its values. A society that includes among its
ideals decency and truth will reflect these in its forms of expression; and
so, by the same token, a totalitarian society will shape the language to its
own devices. There is, in short, a totalitarian "style" of speaking and
writing, directly related to the principles of control and manipulation that

109

characterize the totalitarian society in its more obvious political features as well.

This first premise of Orwell's argument is joined by another, no less fundamental one, namely, that language is also closely tied to thinking— that thoughts or ideas do not just spring up in the mind, but adapt themselves to the words and forms of language that are available. In one of his essays, Orwell does suggest that at an elementary level, it may be possible to think without language; but he recognized that in general, thinking *requires* language, and, also, from its side, that language always reflects the thinking of the speaker. What this means practically is that at the level both of the individual and of society as a whole, the patterns of speaking and writing available—that is, language—directly influence the ideas and thoughts that users of the language may have. Thinking, in other words, does not simply come to the individual, as created by him out of nothing. Rather, the thoughts an individual ''has'' depend on what the language can accommodate. And insofar as the language available has previously been shaped for a specific purpose—for example, as the language had been shaped by a culture or government as a technological tool to be applied in reaching certain political goals—then the mind of the individual, his internal life and freedom to think what he might even then believe are his own thoughts, will be limited to that same extent. In this sense, thinking is confined by language.

These two principles are precisely what Newspeak, the language of *1984,* presupposes as it serves the goals of totalitarianism. In the appendix to *1984,* Orwell describes in detail the structure of Newspeak in its three parts. The first of these—the ''A-Vocabulary''—is a group of common words, composed mainly of simple nouns that refer to concrete objects: so, for example, the words *knife* or *chair.* Such words allow the ordinary business of everyday life to go on, but at an elementary level, with no room for ambiguity or connotation: for every word there is only one kind of thing it can refer to, and that thing is a tangible object. There is no opportunity—no space—left by these words for thinking around or beyond the objects they refer to, or for describing those objects in other terms. Verbs and adjectives, moreover, are derived from these same nouns; so, for example, there is no separate word for ''cut''; the word *knife* is simply used as a verb, as in ''knife me a slice of bread.'' The effect of this usage is two-fold: first, to have the language center on nouns, which are, as *things,* passive; and second, to limit the possibilities of talking—thinking—beyond objects that are in plain view, restricting all thought about them to their simplest purpose of function. If people do not have the means of talking or thinking about other possibilities—and so about the *idea* of possibility—they will be more likely to accept the world around them as given. And this is, quite exactly, what a totalitarian system hopes for from its citizens: that they should live entirely in the present, with no impulse to imagine alternatives, whether in the past—through memory— or in the future, through possibility.

The second part of Newspeak, the "B-Vocabulary," consists of a group of words used for political or social purposes. These are compound words (also usually nouns) made up out of simple words that are joined together in a way that obscures the original meaning of the simpler words. Orwell calls these terms "telescoped" words. The purpose of such terms is to make complicated ideas as simple as the words of the "A-Vocabulary," and thus to preclude questions that might be asked about them. So, for example, Orwell cites "joycamp"—the word in Newspeak that stands for "forced labor camp." The compound word compresses—and alters—the true description of the camp into something quite different; it becomes an easily managed token that has the effect of concealing its actual reference. The telescoping here is meant to draw attention away both from the individual words that make up the compound and from the things those words stand for; it is, beyond that, meant to challenge the assumption that the individual words stand for anything by themselves: their meaning is determined here by their function which is in turn determined by an impersonal and authoritative writer. It is a fact of human psychology, Orwell believes, that if a "forced labor camp" is called a "joycamp" often enough and loudly enough, this is how people will begin to think and to feel about it.

The third part of Newspeak—the "C-Vocabulary"—consists of a group of words to which only specialists of different sorts, for example, scientists, have access; this is the vocabulary they use in carrying on and describing their work. Such specialization of language has the effect, on the one hand, of excluding the public from the language, of making certain that they will understand nothing about it; on the other hand, of making the scientists themselves feel that their work is unrelated to the basic life of the community and the issues involved there. Their work, in other words, is to be kept quite separate from political questions (for example); thus the technicians, too, although advanced in one part of their thinking, are also kept under social control by a process of isolation.

These conditions, taken as a whole, may seem quite fanciful and imaginary, an unlikely picture of either language or society. But there is enough realistic in them to bring home to us once again that *1984* is not a more fantasy. For one thing, it seems clear that if language ever *did* take the form of Newspeak, it would indeed be difficult for the users of the language to step outside it, to think thoughts other than those prefabricated for them. There is quite simply no space left in the narrow lines of Newspeak for imagination, for shadings of meaning, for figures of speech like metaphor or irony: language is flattened out, taken out of its historical setting, set apart even from nature itself. Like hammers and nails, words here are to have only specific and limited practical uses; these can be directly known not only by the user but by anybody else, and so there are checks, both inside and outside, on usage. Words can, in short—like hammers and nails—be controlled; and, like hammers and nails, they give the impression even to their users that there is nothing more then their one immediate use that can be done with them.

Second, as with other aspects of *1984,* this view of language is not only imaginary: Orwell himself already had evidence of its presence, and the evidence has if anything increased since. When a phrase like the "Final Solution" is used to designate murder or genocide; when a government can call the destruction of a town or village "pacification"—a term familiar to Orwell from World War II (and familiar to citizens of the United States, more recently, in Viet Nam), or when a government can make up the phrase "revenue enhancement" as a substitute for "tax"; when new abbreviations or acronyms are constantly introduced to take the place of words and their histories, moving to make language itself an instrument of policy; and when, from a different direction, the technical language of specialists becomes increasingly unintelligible to the public—then we already have a clear anticipation of what the world of *1984* would be like and what the death of language promises.

What is at stake in these different appearances, moreover, is not only language in its everyday use: the situation of literature in such a setting is closely tied to the other, and is, if anything, even more precarious. Orwell argues repeatedly that totalitarianism and literature are incompatible: if you have one, you cannot have the other. Literature requires freedom, not only the appearance of it but the reality—where the individual writer is himself able to judge what the facts are, what is important about them or not, and which of their associations he wants to preserve or to enlarge. Writing, in this sense, entails a constant series of choices and decisions by the writer. Totalitarianism, in contrast, as it implies external control of both collective and individual memory, also moves to control the imagination. Not only the material for writing but the act of writing itself comes to originate outside the writer—a removal that cripples the writer. Politics, we know from experience, may call for sharp reversals of policies and even of ideals; psychologically, let alone morally—and so, also, literarily—the writer is incapable of such forced changes and inconsistencies.

Here again, moreover, Orwell could point to evidence that the times had provided. So far as any authentic literature came out of Nazi Germany or has emerged from Soviet Russia, it has been a literature of opposition—by writers who managed, at least until their writings became public, to escape the control of the regimes. In a perverse way, those governments have in fact taken literature quite seriously, expending needed resources on censorship and the control of individual writers, trying to make sure that the world of literary possibility conformed to their own versions of actuality. (A striking but not atypical example of this is the report we have of Stalin himself making a late-night phone call to the writer Boris Pasternak, trying to learn from Pasternak whether the poet Mandelstam had or had not, at an earlier gathering, recited a derogatory poem about Stalin: Mandelstam survived this inquiry, but he was to die anyway, not long afterward, in Stalin's Gulag.)

To be sure, the description of this imaginary but not only imaginary future still leaves the question of what can be done to avoid the death of language, to prevent Newspeak from taking over. And here again, we have to take seriously the possibility implied by Orwell, that finally this issue may be out of our hands altogether—that just as technological and political developments outstrip the wishes or actions of individual people, so the future of language and writing may also be beyond the control of individuals. There is no ignoring the fact, for example, that the mass media (radio and television in particular, but also newspapers, magazines, and books) have become increasingly centralized and homogenized, that is, based on someone else's prescriptions of what people will—or should—want to read or hear. There is thus, even without overt censorship, a series of controls on public writing and language. On the other hand, language differs from other aspects of culture in at least one respect: that each person, finally, has to use it individually. It is I—or you—who actively have to say or to write the words we use, and who are in a position, then, at least to *try* to control that use of it. If there is any place where the individual is free to decide or to choose, then, surely it is here, in the words or ideas we express. And in one of his most often quoted essays, "Politics and the English Language," written a few years before *1984*, Orwell offers advice about how this freedom may be best put to use. What he says there, in the six "rules" he lists, may sound too simple to be effective: he urges, for example, the importance of avoiding metaphors or other figures of speech that we are accustomed to seeing in print—that is, clichés; and the reason here is, simply, that when we use clichés, we are thinking not our own, but someone else's thoughts. Or again, he urges that whenever we have a choice in writing between a long word or phrase and a shorter one, we should choose the shorter one: the additional—unnecessary—length of the other could be used to obscure the actual meaning of the words and thus to serve other purposes: to give weight that the meaning itself would not carry, to give emotive effect to the words that they would not have by themselves. "Good prose", Orwell writes, "is like a window pane": it should enable the reader to see through it to the object, not to set up detours or to disguise the object. The other rules he mentions are of much the same sort, but it is the last of the six that, in conclusion, I call special attention to: "Break any of these rules," he warns his reader, "sooner than say anything outright barbarous."

To be sure, we may not always be aware that we *are* abusing language; we are so accustomed to its patterns, so much inside them, that it is not easy to stay alert to the effects they have on us and our meanings. Orwell, disciplined as he was, himself admits that he could hardly avoid violating his own rules (including, we may suppose, his last one). But if we listen to Orwell, both in *1984* and in his other writings, we know at least that language can reflect—or even cause—political and moral wrongs, and that the consequences of ignoring this possibility or of not taking it seriously will be important for us individually and for the culture more generally. We know, too, partly *because* of Orwell, that in the complex technological society we inhabit, there are pressures, sometimes evident, sometimes invisible, that are pushing us in a direction where language is used to limit, not to enlarge, thinking and imagination. The recognition of such influence is no guarantee against its consequences—but without that awareness, there would be no defense, and little hope, at all. So we may see even well after the year 1984 the possibility still of avoiding Orwell's *1984.*

14

Virtue as a Literary Form
Orwell's Art

Good prose is like a window pane.
—George Orwell

I

There is wisdom as well as foolishness in the moods of fashion, and both qualities have affected the critical estimates of George Orwell's work. His novels, it seems now, have found their place. The best-known of them, *1984* and *Animal Farm* (something *like* a novel), are period pieces; intended didactically, they would challenge only until their lessons had been memorized—and it requires both energy and malice to forget today that social action moved by the promise of human perfectibility often succeeds in swallowing itself perfectly whole; that "communist" Russia is not (and never was) so communal after all, and that the conciseness of technological advances provides a ready vehicle for totalitarianism. Even before 1984, that novel of Orwell's threw a shadow almost as mannered as Edward Bellamy's *Looking Backward,* which conceived an improbably benign and later year, 2000. The future has been moving too quickly into the present for the most radical science fiction to surprise the contemporary reader as science *or* fiction. What is startling about even an apocalyptic prediction, the reader might ask, if the one article of faith binding him asserts that everything is possible?

At least in parts, the four earlier novels—*Burmese Days, A Clergyman's Daughter, Coming Up for Air,* and *Keep the Aspidistra Flying*—deserve better than the critics have given them, but not so much better as to make an effective difference. Portraits of the artist as he becomes one, they include sceptical, occasionally lavish scenes of life in Burma where Orwell served for five years in the colonial police, and of the class-conscious, still imperial England to which he returned after quitting that job in disgust, with few possessions or expectations other than the decision that he would be a writer. In these novels, too, a barely disguised literal assertiveness obtrudes. Orwell could not, it seems, just conceive a fictional character, display it in motion; he had also to see through it, to find for it a place among the moral ambivalences which a hyperactive sensibility revealed to him even in the mechanics of everyday commonplace. He was not, he confessed in a letter to his friend Julian Symons, "a real novelist anyway." Disinterested, often harsh when judging his own work (at least one of the early novels, he later commented, should never have been published), he could or would not, in writing them, leave himself and the claims of conscience out.

The argument for Orwell's stature as a writer soon turns, then, to his nonfiction—although there again, fashion has worked to pass him by. Subtlety is the rage, and things (how *were* those Victorian philosophers Gilbert and Sullivan so canny about the dawning self-consciousness?) are "seldom what they seem." To understand the designs of a novelist or a politician or a general, one must have uncovered the psychological substructure; to assess the lines of social movement, political reaction, or artistic innovation, the logic of world history must have been settled beforehand. In the terms of such analysis, what is revealed by appearance as obvious or evident becomes impertinence. And to Orwell, the light of indirection was hardly to be preferred to darkness; he would cite many examples of how the one serves as well as the other to cloak ideology and self-interest. A more honest day's work would be to find—and to leave— things alone; and the instrument with which Orwell set out to accomplish this in his nonfiction was an immoderate eye for fact: for what could be *seen* in the Spanish Civil War, as opposed to what partisans of the time said was occurring there; for what it was *to be* down and out in Paris and London, in the industrial and mining town of Wigan or in a boys' preparatory school—in their differences from what the society responsible for these institutional arrangements would have the public find in them.

The reverence for fact, however, itself suggests congruent defects of quality. *Homage to Catalonia* is a generous book, the least impeachable first-hand account of the Spanish Civil War; the faces encountered in Orwell's reports from a Lancashire mine or from his walks along the

Thames Embankment settle permanently in the viewer's resolve. But the discourse of photographs is fixed in the flat lines of historical context. It no longer offers even the promise of tragic "pity and fear" to hear that Russia, anticipating a social revolution which it could not control, subverted the Spanish Republican government; or that the prosperity of the upper classes in Europe's "liberal" civilization of Orwell's youth had been paid for with deprivation for others. The claims may bear retelling—but hardly as fact or news.

Yet the impression persists, beyond such limitations, that Orwell is an important writer, an unusually resourceful craftsman of language and representation. What remains to support that impression, if we continue the recital of his work, will be found in his "smaller writings"—the four volumes of items of so many different kinds and qualities: book reviews, personal letters, Letters to the Editor, letters to *his* editors, and so on.* And, in fact, a number of essays appear among these leavings which generously support the impression of a remarkable power. Those essays are as perfect as any written in this century: the principle of moral action which animates them is no less resonant than in the most compelling essays of Lawrence; their intuition of the movement of the writer's persona, as keen as that in Borges. A number of them are formally quite conventional. Even those, however, reflect certain of the innovations in others which mark off virtually a new genre—a revision of the neat structural closures of the conventional essay into the looser but more adhesive representations of fictional prose; they effect, in the end, an original conjunction of literary means. In accomplishing this, they also join what will be seen as disparate elements of Orwell's character as a writer—and it is important, both for Orwell's work and aside from it, that we should understand how these conjunctions are made.

One structural feature in particular separates the form of Orwell's essays from that of the essay which has been a characteristic presence in English literature of the last three centuries: the role of the author in the animation or action of the work. The claim of a possible variety in that role is not meant to suggest that for the work on one side of the distinction

---

* *The Collected Essays, Journalism and Letters of George Orwell*, ed. Sonia Orwell and Ian Angus (New York, 1968).

the author's presence is evident, on the other, not: even the most impersonal writing will include this much of the design at its source. But the
figure of the author may strike various postures within the circumference
of a plot, and significant differences in this respect mark Orwell's writing.
Typically, in the essay's traditional form—for varied examples, in Samuel
Johnson, in William Hazlitt, or Virginia Woolf—the reader quickly recognizes that the ''I'' who speaks from the essay is meant to be literally
identified with the author. The state of affairs reconstructed in the writing,
furthermore, has been previously determined by him and framed with a
conclusion to which the reconstruction points: an experience leaves an
impression; the work of another writer strikes a chord; past abstractions
call for (or against) elaboration. The ''I'' of the essayist appears in the
telling of such occasions as it would in a conversational report of historical
or speculative event: the author, to one side—*himself* a fact—recounting
a body of external data, the objects of his experience. The division between the writer and what he writes about is made plain as he segregates
his data in two groups: a factual base—places, events, quotations; and
the author's response—inferences, metaphors, judgments. The reader is
invited to join the writer in viewing the factual base, and then to match
responses with him.

In the most distinctive of Orwell's essays (I refer here for examples to
''Shooting an Elephant'' and ''A Hanging''), the role of the author is
notably different. His presence in the movement of the essays is evident;
it is clear, moreover, that the details of his descriptions, even of his own
part in them, are recounted as historical events. But the retelling also
incorporates an unusual feature of reflexivity. The ''I,'' the omnipresent
figure of the author who traditionally moves at will within the essay,
appears here not as master in that house but as one of its occupants. The
perception which discerned the events told lingers not as memory or
theory but in a virtual and constant present. The essayist addresses his
audience less as a second observer of a scene laid open by his own sharper
eye than as a participant in the scene. The author is a persona dramatis—
part of that persona, of course, being a writer. Like any member of the
cast, the viewpoint he opens to the reader is limited and determined within
the work—one among the others. The reader thus gains access not to an
independent world, not even to the author's settled habit or reflection of

119

mind. He is admitted to a collective, still articulate process of the essay itself, a process initiated by particular objects or events which only later, through a transaction between the reader and the author, became a whole. The essayist, reflexively, appears as a character in the essay.

So, for example, Orwell relates an incident in "Shooting an Elephant" which might have been detachedly retold as historical narrative. During his service in Burma, an elephant that belonged to a villager ran amok, first leaving the village and then returning and killing someone in it. The elephant finally wanders out to a nearby field. His owner, who might have calmed him, had set out in the wrong direction; there is no hope that he can be recalled in time to help. Orwell sends for a rifle, intending to use it, he tells the reader, only if the elephant goes on the attack again. But in the meantime the people of the village have gathered, and when the rifle arrives, Orwell faces a spontaneous conspiracy—their expectation of sport, on the one hand (not least of all, the possibility that the elephant would get *him*), and of food, on the other. He shoots the elephant, he writes, knowing at the time that it is unnecessary, knowing the economic loss it means for the owner—having discovered that in the role of master he is yet ruled by his subjects, that he has killed the elephant "only to avoid making a fool of myself."

In "A Hanging," the detail of narrative action is simpler yet. A native is to be hanged in the yard of a regional prison in Burma. Orwell follows the prisoner on the short walk from the condemned cells to the gallows: a dog breaks into the procession and jumps up to lick the prisoner's face; the prisoner sidesteps a puddle to avoid getting wet. The prisoner mounts the platform, chanting a last prayer; the hangman pulls the lever that releases the drop. A few macabre jokes break the tension as the small assembly disperses. Orwell finds himself laughing loudly at the jokes. "The dead man," he closes the essay, "was a hundred yards away."

As it must be for any single object of art, a report on the effectiveness of these short essays inevitably misses their art. How, especially, can a reader recount by the elements of a response the unusual sense of dramatic integrity that he claims for the whole? But a ground for the response can be remarked in the summaries given. It is more than an accidental feature of their detail that we recognize from the expectation of the crowd, from the prisoner sidestepping a puddle, that the author himself is not freed even with the writing from the events he describes. To be sure, the abrasiveness of the events contributes to this persistence. But the reflexive posture of the author adds a factor of adhesion which the events would not by themselves. The author's "I" asserts only as much in the way of a presence as is defined in the expression of the other "I's" who appear: we hear nothing in the way of obiter dictum or self-justification; no representation of the author acting in the present to resolve the past into abstraction; no hope of a spectator's absolution which detachment from the context, shared between the writer and reader, might bring to each. There is a great equality in the distribution of power among the characters: Orwell, the villagers, the elephant, the prison guards, the prisoner who is hanged, and finally the reader—an equality, the absence of which, in these particular essays, was precisely what had set the events they describe and thus the essays themselves in motion. The writer could as well be the reader, at least to the extent that any reader of literary fiction discovers piecemeal elements of his identity in that representation. And surely it is some such quality of introjection, of a cumulative adhesion to the reader's self by aspects of the characters who appear before him, that enforces the lure of fiction and distinguishes its accomplishment from the comfortable disinterest evoked by the separation in the traditional essay between the objects written about and whoever is writing (or reading) about them. Orwell the author is constantly and by design also one of the author's objects; the invitation to the reader is no less modestly divided.

Not all of Orwell's essays are so equably drawn around the figure of the author as the two that have been outlined; some of them follow more closely the standard conventions by which the author and his reader are separated both from each other and from the events reviewed in the writing. But it is rare, even in these, that the reflexive quality by which the author assigns to himself the agency of character and to the reader a proportionately extended invitation does not come out. This is the case, for example, in "Such, Such Were the Joys," where Orwell rehearses memories of his prep school—a part of his life which he was in historical fact reluctant to revive; it is true even of the polemical piece "Benefit of the Clergy," in which Orwell attacks artists in general and Salvador Dali in particular for assuming the right to stylistic carte blanche: freedom to say anything at all, so long as it is said well. The former of these essays is retrospective, the latter, more openly didactic—but in them both the figure of the author is represented in the same terms that bind the other objects of his scrutiny: his judgments about events long past in the life of a schoolboy and about the extra-artistic obligations of the artist are judgments on Orwell himself in the virtual time of the writing. Orwell as author is still the "new" boy wetting his bed until he is beaten out of the habit; Orwell himself expresses the moral spirit of art as he separates his disgust at what Dali says from praise of Dali as a draughtsman. The persona of the editorial "I" never fails to speak—but it speaks about Orwell under the same constraints that limit the other objects or characters or events of the narrative. The essayist quite explicitly denies himself the "benefit of clergy."

In this sense, it seems, the same defects that mar Orwell's novels—the conscientious intrusion of the author and the subordination of artistic license to the restrictions of fact—add an unexpected resource to the conventional form of the essay. It is as though the impulses underlying those appearances would always for Orwell distort or strain the medium of the novel; only after a long search had they located a passage that would admit both Orwell's bulky grasp of the detail of experience and the moral incentive for the judgment which sustained that grasp. In the essays mentioned, these elements which would in other forms (as in Orwell's own fiction) violate the even circle of art, redefine that circle through the status assumed by the author as one among the members of the essay's cast. This democratic appearance is too constant a feature to be accidental; elliptically, it recalls the reference of our title to the principle of decency as an item first and more openly of Orwell's politics—second and more fundamentally, of Orwell's art.

II

The word *decency* itself sounds quaint on the contemporary ear, and it is instructive because of this to note that Orwell returns to it in moments when the "I" who is a character in his essays is most convincingly Orwell himself. The formal principle of decency is a constant presence in his writing. Thus, explaining his decision to fight in Spain, where he was later severely wounded, he writes: "If you had asked me why I had joined the militia I should have answered: 'To fight against fascism,' and if you had asked me what I was fighting *for,* I should have answered, 'Common decency.' " Ideology itself is subordinate to the principle, he argues in *The Road to Wigan Pier*: "So far as my experience goes, no genuine working man grasps the deeper implications of socialism. Often, in my opinion, he is a truer Socialist than the orthodox Marxist, because he does remember, what the other so often forgets, that Socialism means justice and common decency." In his essay on Dickens, Orwell's criticism of Dickens as a social thinker is mitigated by one large qualification: "His radicalism is of the vaguest kind, and yet one always knows that it is there. That is the difference between being a moralist and a politician. He has no constructive suggestions, not even a clear grasp of the nature of the society he is attacking, only an emotional perception that something is wrong. All he can finally say is, 'Behave decently,' which . . . is not so shallow as it sounds." And in a letter soon afterwards, to Humphrey House (11 April 1940), he identifies Dickens' commitment as his own: "The thing that frightens me about modern intelligentsia is their inability to see that human society must be based on common decency, whatever the political and economic forms may be."

In one obvious sense, of course, such judgments do not move very far. Who, after all, would dispute the claims of decency? Who, before that, would bother to mention them? In this appeal to something resembling a moral intuition, furthermore, we undoubtedly hear an echo of the code of values bred to English upper-class character which Orwell himself often contested but never escaped. ("Then are you a gentleman?" asks the manager of the "Spike" at Lower Binfield, in which Orwell playing the role of tramp was spending the night. "I suppose so," Orwell replied— reluctantly conceding the undeniable.)

So far as I have been able to find, moreover, Orwell never says what meaning he assigns to the principle of decency, or gives reasons for placing it at the basis of moral, let alone dramatic, judgment. There is evidence that he was quite uninterested in such questions. ("It is the sort of thing," he writes about a section of Bertrand Russell's book *Human Knowledge,* "that makes me feel that philosophy should be forbidden by law.") To be sure, the challenges to decency in effect are named and everywhere: hypocrisy, the double standard, the battles in Everyman be-tween Sancho Panza and Don Quixote, suggest a Manichean presence which threatens any good of which men or societies are capable. The reports of that threat are constant, and even the fact that Orwell was acutely tuned to its appearances might be viewed by the reader as inadequate compensation for the monotony of their enumeration. This is one theme that never escapes him.

But his reiteration of the principle and its instances makes a deliberate point. For surely, among the issues affecting moral judgment, the first and largest is not which principle shall rule that judgment, but whether any principle governs it at all. The latter question Orwell saw as the most serious casualty of the subtlety of contemporary social analysis. In the attentiveness of such analysis to the causal sequence of social process, to tracing and anticipating its consequences, it had largely ignored the question of the form of the process as a whole—what the process was and why it evolved as it had. Lacking the coherence which recognition of this question confers, and skewed by the dogmatic terms of ideology, the appearance of the process would necessarily be fragmented and partial. This accounts, as Orwell reviews the evidence, for the bad judgment and self-serving apologetics displayed by his contemporaries among the "intellegentsia": in their refusal to acknowledge Stalinism for the barbarism it was, in their defeatism in the early days of World War II, in their inability to find a difference between the opposing sides in that war. And if Orwell was uninterested in the derivation of the specific principle that might more justly determine a perspective on such cases, he never forgot and intended that his reader should never forget that it is with the principle of moral design that any analytic perspective begins and ends. Ultimately, intellectual and artistic neutrality or disinterest are fictions, and vicious ones at that. Only by admitting the role of moral principle in perception as well as in judgment does the world, for Orwell, become intelligible.

That principle, furthermore, if it has any claims at all, holds in general. Thus, for the writer, it acquires a reflexive or self-implicating quality which presents the writer himself as an important instance. The world of fact possesses for Orwell a dramatic unity which the form of his essays is designed to reenact. The facts displayed at any moment within those unities—the actuality or the representation—necessarily include the eye that discriminates them. Decency, Orwell might have argued, could not have it otherwise than that the written word should apply the same standards to its writer and to its reader that it lives by itself. The objects and events of history are nothing without the eye that joins or separates them; they *require* discrimination. And as this process of discrimination ought itself to appear in their representation, so also the persons of the writer and of the reader he addresses. Drama, we know independently, extracts from all of its characters a confession of finitude: a common incompleteness which is then tested and measured by a general principle of virtue. It is a last and binding irony of his art that this measurement which constantly forces its way beyond the artistic limits of detachment in Orwell's attempts at conventional fiction, confers, through the same excess, dramatic power on the medium of the essay, which has not traditionally been a vehicle for drama at all.

The American writer to whom Orwell as essayist bears the strongest resemblance is Thoreau—a comparison that starts to their common disadvantage. Orwell was never at home with the Burmese peasants or the coal miners of Wigan or the English hoboes to whom he committed himself as a writer; the likeness that comes to mind is in a contemporary account which tells of Thoreau interrupting the austerities of Walden Pond to sneak home for some of his mother's pies. The art in both cases, it seems clear, was consciously informed, however spontaneous the germ. We find in the work of each a representation of the author that the author scarcely realized in his own person. But the integrity of the author who is a character in the written work is, in both writers, confirmed. The moral impulse linked almost physiologically to the eye for fact, the balking at the over-subtle consciousness, the reflexive "I" that counts itself among the objects of action in the writing, the drama located in events by their very discrimination as events: this summary humility, this uncommon decency acting on the world discerned, the representations of the two writers share. But then, the need to which Orwell answers, beyond his art, is also a bond; that there should be a knowing recluse who might penetrate the surrounding mass of artifice. Walden Pond, after all, is a metaphor of contrast. The contrast it argues, furthermore, has in subsequent history widened rather than diminished, at least by the difference between pencil making in Concord and the coal pits of Wigan. And if the metaphor seems also to have altered, the change is, for Orwell, in the fashion of idiom, not in substance.

125

15

Human Nature and Political Artifact

The state comes into existence for the sake of mere life; it continues to exist for the sake of the good life.

—*Aristotle*

There is a key in human anatomy to the anatomy of the apes.

—*Marx*

It is understandable that attempts to justify the forms of political organization found themselves on concepts of human nature. To have located such a basis is to make the question of what political organization is desirable a matter simply of logic. So, for example: "Since people are by nature individualistic and possessive, it is futile to legislate that property should be held in common." An objection to the conclusions of such arguments, on the grounds perhaps that one would find it more congenial to live in a society in which property was held in common, becomes then a suggestion that the institutions of society would be more congenial if people were different from what they are—a reasonable but not very informative claim.

Indeed, it seems that any attempt to answer the questions to which political philosophy traditionally turns, as they ask what political structures and instruments are desirable, *must* invoke (wittingly or not) a conception or theory of human nature, a portrait of the individual who is to constitute the body politic. Any proposal for a form of government will be either arbitrary or not. If it is not arbitrary, it will speak about what people can (as well as ought to) do in the state and by means of the state. And it is unlikely, if not impossible, that these conclusions can be reached in ignorance of human capacities and dispositions. It may be extravagant to argue that a vote on fluoridating the city water inevitably conceals a theory of human nature; but it is clear that decisions which have a strong purchase on policies of the commonwealth (for example, as they regulate the economy, or the role of the state in education, or even fluoridation) often *do* rest precisely on such theories.

It is indisputable, in any event, that many political philosophers, quite different in other respects, have openly sought or covertly assumed a basis for their doctrines in a conception of human beings as they *really* are. This attentiveness on the part of political theory has produced a tradition according to which any conception of human nature presupposes an account of that nature outside or prior to the state, and the rationale for this strategy is not difficult to see. Surely, the rationale goes, human beings *in* society have been formed and influenced by its institutions. One cannot be certain, then, whether a desire for property (for example) is intrinsic or whether it has been imposed, against or despite human nature, by society's institutions. The only means of determining which of these is the case (so the argument) is by stripping away the accretions built up by civilization and history, by locating human beings outside the political structure: there we see them as they are ''naturally.'' To know what they are like in nature is, then, also to learn both why they first entered the state and what form the state should have.

This pattern of argument will be familiar to readers of social contract theories, from Glaucon's in the *Republic* to the accounts of Hobbes, Locke, and Rousseau. It has reappeared more recently in an attenuated form, which like any good caricature brings out the central (and problematic) features of the original. I refer with this description to attempts such as those of Robert Ardrey and Konrad Lorenz* to draw certain morals for political philosophy not only from what human beings are outside the state, but from what *nonhuman* beings are (also, of course, outside the state). It must be acknowledged that the latter additional step does make a kind of sense—as much, at least, as the premise on which it is based. If, after all, to know what people are naturally, outside the body politic, is to understand more than one would by observing them inside the state, how much more could we learn from their still more original or ''natural''

---

* R. Ardrey, *African Genesis; A Personal Investigation into the Animal Origin and Nature of Man* (New York, 1961) and *The Territorial Imperative: A Personal Inquiry into the Animal Origins of Property and Nations* (New York, 1966); K. Lorenz, *On Aggression* (New York, 1966).

existence? And this we find out, the recent argument goes, by collecting evidence concerning the early, prehuman stages of homo sapiens and the animals which evolved parallel with him.

Admittedly, the theorists who argue along these lines differ among themselves (sometimes even within themselves) as to where we must go to find evidence of this prepolitical nature. Hobbes, with his spectacular version of the war of nature, acknowledges that the evidence for that war comes principally from what he had seen of human beings *in* society at the time. Look at the malevolence of people when they have the benefits of a state and culture—Hobbes invites his reader—and imagine the mischief they would be guilty of without them. And the immediate methodological issue is not whether extrapolation from England in the seventeenth century to the state of nature is justified; what is relevant to the argument here is Hobbes's recognition of the difficulty of locating evidence about human nature as it (really) is in nature, *aside* from what we know of it in the state. A similar admission appears in Locke's *Second Treatise,* where Locke bases his version of "natural man" on an analogy between individual persons and individual nations (as they were in Locke's time, but also, as it turns out, in our own). Nations, governed by no law, fall victim to those which are self-seeking and powerful—and so it must be also among people when *they* have no external hindrance. Again, Locke surely conceives of the state of nature as historical—and, as historical, well in the past. But he concedes that the evidence on which our knowledge of that past is founded is evidence in the present.

One reason for such cautionary tones is surely the one already cited. For, if we do not have access to human nature outside the state as evidence of what it really is (outside or inside the state), then we can only construct a theory of what it is on what we know of its appearance within the state. And so far as *this* is the evidence we rely on, assertions about human nature claim no more—although they seem to—than that human beings are originally and natively simply what we observe them to be presently and apparently. (This was the onus of Hume's criticism of the classical social contract theorists—and his argument has lost none of its edge.)

There may be, however, a second and more significant reason for the use by social contract theorists of evidence from the present to reach back to the past. The classical theorists themselves do not make much of it, and the contemporary writers named ignore it entirely—the assumption that *natural* behavior is an item of *privileged* evidence in the search for a conception of human nature and, in turn, as a basis for political policies and structures. This is, it seems, a straightforward example of what has been named the ''genetic fallacy''—the assumption that, by identifying the origins of a phenomenon, one also identifies its function or value. In the case of Ardrey and Lorenz, the assumption is made that if we know why the state *comes into* existence then we also know why it continues to exist—that the reasons people have for originally entering the state persist as their reasons for remaining in the state.

The reason for regarding this assumption as an instance of the genetic fallacy should be evident; namely, that even if we could ascertain what human beings were like outside any political organization, or what it was that first led them to the state, or how their forebears and animal relatives lived (or continue to), that information affords no *privileged* view of human nature, but no more than *another* one. It is undoubtedly the case that human beings, as they existed or might exist outside the state, have something in common with human beings after they enter the state: in either role, they appear in a context of needs and capacities, on the one hand, and of conditions externally imposed, on the other. These two variables, however, alter in time; but unless we can *show* that one particular time is more privileged than any other, it is arbitrary to claim that a view of their prepolitical existence reveals human nature as it *really* is, as opposed to what is disclosed *in* the state. It makes as much sense, in other words, to say that we can settle on a theory of human nature by observing human conduct within a specific political setting as it does to say that we can find out what human nature is by observing people outside of *any* political setting. We may—possibly—in pursuing the latter course, escape the political context; but the aim of such searches is to go beyond *all* contexts, to see human beings as they would be if *no* external conditions affected them. And that hope, of course, is vain.

Another way of putting this objection recalls the epigraph cited above from *Politics,* in which Aristotle disputes the assumption that human nature is constant for all the stages of its development and no matter what the external conditions—economic, intellectual, aesthetic—are. The latter assumption might turn out to be true (and the alternative—that humans in the state is quite different from what they would be outside it—false). But if the former is true, it is hardly true a priori; and if it is not true a priori, then we may expect to be given some evidence for it. Works such as Ardrey's and Lorenz's make no serious effort to do this. Ardrey, for example, arguing from evidence of murder in early human remains, concludes that people now (as well as then) are by nature aggressive. And it is enough for him to point to the territorial possessiveness of primitive man and even of his simian relations to argue that in modern times, too, this instinct is dominant.

The implications of the supposed constancy of an "animal" nature in human political existence are made quite clear: nationalism, for example, becomes a natural rather than an accidental or historical principle of political organization; the natural tendency to disorder in society permanently requires the institutions of discipline, a police force, for example; the privacy of property is a given which any rational political structure must acknowledge; and so on. Behind these specific claims persist the broader, theoretical ones: that human nature is most evident—truest—in its primitive state, and that it is, subsequently, immutable. Aristotle's statement challenges the latter thesis as it argues that the reasons why the state comes into existence are not—or, at least, *may* not be—the reasons for its continued existence. The denial of Aristotle's claim can be based either on a priori grounds (in which case we may choose as easily to ignore it as not) or by some strange blending of a priori reasoning with empirical elements (about which I say a word below). In *either* event, and whatever the conclusions reached, claims made about what human nature *really* is do not have the status, as Ardrey and Lorenz imply, of simple empirical descriptions.

Notice that I have not been arguing that the specific portrait of human nature as aggressor, as drawn by Ardrey or Lorenz, is mistaken. The objections I have raised are methodological; they would hold against *any* account which attempts to deduce, solely from details in the life of primitive people or of primates, human nature as it "really" is. Some accounts that follow this pattern are quite different in their conclusions from the ones cited—for example, that of Ashley Montague,* who sees people as

---

* A. Montague, *Anthropology and Human Nature* (Boston, 1957).

130

(by nature) cooperative and unaggressive. I have not even been arguing that either the kind of evidence or the evidence itself employed in the accounts cited is irrelevant to the questions which they think they are answering. It seems clear, in fact, that, if those questions are to be answered at all, such evidence will be relevant: but—and here the story's moral—whatever the relevance of such data, they will never be *sufficient* to yield by themselves a conception of what human nature "really" is.

A final, and obvious, question emerges from this sequence of argument. For even if a logical discontinuity between empirical data and a theory of human nature were assumed, the question is still unanswered of what the connection *is* between them—in short, how a theory of human nature is even to be conceived. One aspect of that derivation has already been specified. If a theory of human nature can rely on no privileged context of evidence, still there are items of evidence—in the varieties of human action and evaluation. These items are not, we have seen, hierarchical; but the political philosopher will be responsible for making an order out of them nonetheless. His task, moreover, does not end there; and in noting this, we may have found the yet unspoken reason why the classical social contract theorists were so ready to take history's name in vain. For even if we assemble all the individual items of evidence about human character, what we have then is still an aggregate—not a theory or concept; and the implications drawn from such evidence can be put only in terms of hypotheticals: for example, that if a state were organized as an absolute monarchy, given certain external conditions it would respond in certain ways. What we do *not* find in this aggregate and its implied hypotheticals is the last step required for a general account of human nature, of what people, within or outside any or all particular political structures, truly are. That step would turn hypothetical statements of "how human beings would act if . . ." into assertions of what human beings are now; and this last step can be taken, it seems, only as we recognize that it involves, beyond the gathering of empirical data, a sense both of human possibility and human value.

I can hardly undertake here to discuss this last element, and indeed that is not my purpose. What I have provided evidence for is a methodological claim that the pertinent question for determining political structure or action is not *whether* a more than empirical feature should be admitted, but *which* one will be; and second, that political theories which think to identify this factor only by viewing human conduct in particular social contexts or, what comes to the same thing, outside of any context are, like any attempt to know what something is when it is unobserved, condemned to futility or misrepresentation. The outlines or ideals of political structure are not given unless they are also taken. If this seems to suggest that political theory and the conception of human nature it presupposes involve, beyond empirical matters of fact, an a priori or subjective ground, we have to allow for the power of suggestion. The fault, in any event, is not in political theorizing or in what we would like to have theories of human nature tell us. Marx, committed by his own precepts and more than almost any other political philosopher to bringing philosophy down from heaven to earth, left it still—where the question of human nature was concerned—someplace in midair. "Why not argue from human conduct back to the apes rather than the other way 'round?" he suggests in the epigraph at the beginning of this essay—and although a question is not an answer, it is not a wrong answer, either.

16

The Body Impolitic

Thinking Thoreau

One cannot expect heroism from a government.
—Stendhal

The role of society's gadfly was perhaps the genius, but certainly (as well) the profession, of Socrates—"... settling here, there, and everywhere, rousing, persuading, reproving. . . ." And even if we recognize that in a state that was wise and just, the gadfly would have found other employment, we may still admit that it is a fortunate society which is sufficiently endowed, even in injustice, to produce a native Socrates. That critic of the state must expect to be patronized or scourged in the public life which his own life and work parody; but only a notably foolhardy public would continue to ignore the irony of this antagonism. A body politic cannot hope to meet often the gadfly's conciliation of disinterest and concern.

Of course, it is not the Socratic evocation of the Greek city-state that Thoreau recreates for America. Walden's shores could not have held a philosopher to whom street corners were metaphysically important: the trees, Socrates reminded Phaedrus, do not speak. And the measurements taken by Thoreau as surveyor, he might have added, could contribute little to a geography of the self. But in the moral commitment of the two men and in their fine eye for fact in political experience, the analogy between both their lives and their works is pointed. Each spun a parable of human freedom around a text provided by his prison cell. Both continued, by way of that parable, to a revolutionary criticism of the legitimacy of the state—and beyond this, to the conclusion that personal autonomy, confirmed for them in the anonymity of their prison cells, marks off a domain within any political self to which the state must remain alien.

Thoreau is undoubtedly available to a broader variety of sensibility than

Socrates: the groundskeeper and Harvard man, the confrere of Emerson who devised a very good pencil—credentials, it seems, to the most contemporary embassies of speculative or applied reason. What could we touch in the American grain if we ignored the resourcefulness of Walden's settler, or the penetrating immediacy of consciousness with which he scanned its history? Writing, for Thoreau, enlarging these elements, was not a description of his encounter with the world; it was itself a moment in the encounter.

His critics have been ready, because of the texture of this synthesis, to write off Thoreau as thinker. Like Socrates with his airy examples of cobbling and dressage and cooking, Thoreau looks a wastrel: two years and two months is no small time in which to observe a pond; and then, one notes the list of economies so extravagantly kept:

```
Outgoes during the first year:
    House.................................................................$28.12–1/2
    Farm one year ......................................................  14.72–1/2
    Food eight months ................................................   8.74
    Clothing, etc., eight months......................................   8.40–3/4
    Oil, etc., eight months ...........................................   2.00
                                                                        ─────────
        In all ........................................................$61.99–3/4
```

A person, the reader might predict, with time to squander and little else to spend.

In fact, of course, Thoreau takes time seriously—more seriously than those around him who approach it only to mark it or to pass it. To "spend a day deliberately as nature" could be wasteful only to someone for whom nothing is ever preserved—held in fief, perhaps, but not saved. In his attentiveness to the present, in the painstaking concern to live within the means of the moment—and more, to celebrate those means—Thoreau is an arch-conservative. If we understand this, forestalling the paradox, we sense also the revolutionary cast of his politics: Thoreau, having located the human difference in the power of an individual to choose his terms of identity and then to live with that choice, admits the price of maintaining this power to include the sacrifice of any of the institutions of state— even those necessary to its existence. The law courts, the legislative assemblies: there is no space large enough or time long enough in the proportions of a political body to take the measure of this original and durable gift; the reverse is more than only true, it demands constant doing.

When Thoreau left Concord jail, he continued on an errand to the shoemaker's which his day in jail had interrupted. His errand was the same; only the world in which he acted had altered. As he writes of it, that day had removed finally the possibility that he would inhabit a commonwealth with his fellows, walking its grounds with them, identifying himself by the legends of its devices. He sees, in moving from this most solicitous of habitats, that if he is to do *himself* justice, if he is to define for himself a place and identity, the means for doing so will not come from outside; it is a case of like being known only to like—and the self, which knows and chooses, is not outside in the state.

Here, indeed, is revolution. As principle is fitted to fact always with something left over for principle to reflect on, so (he writes) action from principle "does not consist wholly with anything which was." And the state, however one judges the reality of political motives or virtues, most certainly *was*. There is, Thoreau finds, a separation—the literal difference of two worlds—between the person who had "traveled much" (though it was in Concord) and the citizen locked up in the local jail. "As they could not reach me," he writes of Concord's citizens, "they had resolved to punish my body, just as boys, if they cannot come against some person against whom they have a spite, will abuse his dog."

The political process, Thoreau thus suggests, acts on a political self— the soldier as he marches to war, the judge who administers the law, the payer of taxes. It can act only around or across the self which assigns (or accepts) these roles and which, as it exercises this power comprises for the individual—*any* individual—a majority of one sufficient for action on complex or delicate matters of state. Each of us inhabits, as Socrates had concluded, a "commonwealth of the mind." The political commonwealth, blind and dull after the nature of instruments, knows nothing of this. We cannot, of course, blame it for the obtuseness of its nature; but neither should that simplicity be mistaken for authenticity or as a justification for its impostures. The state *seems* to make decisions, to act—but this is not more than the deceptive appearance that an idiot may give. One can trace in a democracy the "ayes" and "nays" which converge in its decisions; but these choices are not to be mistaken as decisions made by the *state*.

Clearly enough, the state moves; it is nonetheless the people inhabiting the state who give the motion its impetus, if only by deciding to allow it to proceed. The state proceeds disinterestedly and uninterestedly, responding with its forces, equitably, to the alternatives before it. Responsibility for overseeing its progress thus remains where responsibility begins, in the individuals who lend their names to it.

The matter of assuming that responsibility is not one of sitting in judgment on all of the hindrances which come from political organization. "All systems," we know, "have their frictions," and some such friction—of inconvenience or discomfort—we can live with. But where the machine of state exists for the sake of the friction, where its end is unjust and not simply imprudent, the citizens who acquiesce also affirms: they themselves commit the acts of state, a witting agent so long as they are witting enough only to pay the taxes which nourish its movement. The occasions for Thoreau's essay "On the Duty of Civil Disobedience" were the role of the United States in the Mexican War and the government's sanction of slavery. The motives and ends expressed in those actions, Thoreau argues, were in principle unjust; and with principle, unlike taste, reason can dispute. To accept as a value the human capacity for marking out its own designs is to accept as well the obligation to see where and by whom that principle is violated—a procedure ruled not by taste or inclination, but by the understanding of the principle itself.

Nor, Thoreau argues, do the techniques of the democratic process efface the citizen's responsibility at court. The state must take a constant risk in living with its constituents; citizens are bound in honor both to set the terms of the risk and to keep it alive. The ballot, in fact, deserves no more respect than that accorded any other tokens of gambling. At best, it is a prediction, moved by hope, of what the majority will agree on. Voters in effect leave the outcome of the issue on which they vote to the chance that the side they support will win (or lose). So far as they cut their actions to the measure of that process, they leave unrequited the consequences which follow from it. All that they do about those consequences is to accept them beforehand—whatever these are. And this may not be enough.

"But what," we hear, "if everybody acted on such principle?"—the moral question thrown at Thoreau with the full passion of the moral naif.

"What, after all, of the strength of the polity, its ability to defend, to educate? Can a citizen simply *choose* the laws he will obey?" And Thoreau's answer, surely: "What of it? To defend what? Should a citizen choose to do what he ought not to do?" The issue for him here, and the terms in which he addresses it, are clear. Where policies of the state reflect injustice in principle, asking the citizen (if only by his silence) to be party to them, *his* choice, unaltered, is still between justice and injustice. The state may have its uses; but they are admissible only as they do not constrain the individual to do what he ought not to do. If, to preserve conscience, the state must be opposed—well, this is what must be. It is not the mere life of the state (more than any other item of technology) which is the citizen's responsibility to devise or support, but only its just life: he is first jurist and only second mechanic.

Admittedly, it will be difficult to decide *when* the state has lost its claim to obedience. But this does not differ from the difficulty which figures in the making of *any* ethical choice: and, difficulties and possibilities of error notwithstanding, we make them. As we judge right and wrong elsewhere, Thoreau's argument goes, we may judge it as well in the state: what is crucial is recognition of the parallel. The state exists not for its own good, but for a good of another quality. Its failure, then, will be more than only a practical failure, and Thoreau sees to the end of his thesis as he recognizes the consequences of such failure: "I cannot for an instant recognize as my government that political organization which is the slaves' government also."

Thoreau hardly argues his case or attempts to justify it; but surely this is because the alternative is all too clear, in error as well as in detail. And surely the layman in the twentieth century has had a more sophisticated education in recognizing that alternative than even the expert of 1849: we have a full understanding of what it means to say that the laws of state deserve obedience no matter what they command, that human wisdom expressed individually is inferior to the corporate wisdom of governments. If the bankruptcy of such doctrine was writ large in Thoreau's world, how would we assess the moral sense of our own contemporaries who defend it?

The polity, of course, will reserve its defense to justification by "reasons of state." But as "reasons," these are misnamed; they are, in fact, human reasons dehumanized, designated means only and attesting nothing of the ends with which he must supply them; they are, as Thoreau would have it, not reasons at all. We see this in the "actions" of those through whom the state speaks: civil servants "are as likely to serve the Devil, without *intending* it, as God"; soldiers? "What are they? men at all? or small movable forts or magazines?" Perhaps (so one might attempt their defense) we should admit only that these people have answered a calling, and that that calling serves a purpose. But Thoreau, a constant witness, points unceasingly to the one profession which must precede any other— that of recognizing one's own humanity.

The analogy between Thoreau and Socrates is limited. Socrates, denying the state the right (and power) to censor his actions and thought, still felt himself sufficiently indebted to sacrifice his life for its existence. The state could not force him to behave as it ordered, but he would not deny its right to punish him for refusing—since this, he argued, proposed as a principle, would ensure its destruction. Thus Socrates spurns the opportunity to escape his executioners, giving the state the last power, although not, of course, the last word.

Not for Thoreau, then, this Socratic ideal of the state as parent, whose life is essential to one's own—the other party to an unbreakable contract. To be sure, the hope is evident in what he says that as just people acknowledge the duty of civil disobedience, that fact in itself will be therapeutic for injustice: the state, shamed, may right itself. But he is more sanguine, and perhaps more rigorous, than Socrates in facing other possibilities: that the state's tolerance for shame may be intolerably high; that if the jails should be filled with the righteous members of a society, the state, not through cosmic redress of the moral balance but by a practical failure of resource, may well fall. Thoreau is not unaware of the menace in this eventuality, and it is clear that he does not welcome the prospect. He recognizes, however, that whatever the scope of the dangers, they belong to a lesser order than that of their alternatives. The choice between the live individual and the inanimate corporation does not afford even the semblance of a serious decision.

It requires no great subtlety of conscience or wit to read Thoreau as a contemporary. The issue persists of the conflict between moral and legal obligation—as it sounded, for example, for the citizens of Germany who thought to justify, in terms of the law of state, crimes against "peace and humanity." More immediately, we know that many otherwise willing citizens of the United States regarded the American role in Vietnam as no less a contraversion of conscience than Thoreau did the American war in Mexico. The prospect is in fact constant of state injustice—in civil rights, in economic inequity, in the making of new and other wars. This is not the place to argue for or about individual cases which may or may not fit Thoreau's model for the justification of civil disobedience. The important and live element in Thoreau's conception of the relation between the state and individual is only that such a fit is always possible— and that when it occurs, the course of action which ought to follow is unmistakable. We know this most certainly—here again the crux of Thoreau's very concise argument—if only we consider the alternative to this and the unquestioning submission then implied to the dictates of the state.

In a just state, the conclusion to the argument runs, the just person will also be a good citizen; in a state which is unjust, that role must alter, and as a matter not of inclination, but of obligation. The commonweal indeed has its claims, but they are not limitless. Obligations come from other sources as well. Thoreau, pointing this moral, must surely be an annoyance to any state: no one, and bodies politic less so than most, cherishes reminders of mortality. But then it is true for all the efforts of the gadfly that the irritation which follows its sting is symptomatic, and not only of healing.

17

Hannah Arendt and the
Politics of Evil

In the twentieth century the position of the German Jewish community was to be one of unusual complexity, of powerful ironies and, ultimately, of great disruption and pain. On the one hand, the ideals nourished by the Enlightenment, emerging in the last part of the eighteenth century, and represented in Germany by such figures as Kant, Lessing, and Goethe, had spoken eloquently about the dignity of man, about the principles of civic equality and the inalienable rights shared by all persons. The hopeful statements of these ideals, and the political changes which accompanied them, produced a strong sense of identification on the part of German Jews in the life of their country. By the beginning of the twentieth century, and still more obviously by the time of the First World War, German Jews had a tradition of actively contributing to German culture—in literature and the arts, in the natural and social sciences, in politics. If one extends this brief survey to German as a language and not only to Germany as a political entity, the achievements loom even larger— since we would make room, then, as the present century unfolded, also for the Vienna of Freud and the Prague of Franz Kafka.

And yet, of course, notwithstanding the principles announced by the Enlightenment, despite the achievements of the German Jewish community and the will of many of its members to identify themselves as Germans, the nation and the culture resisted their integration, first in small ways, and then much more purposefully. Why this process went in the direction it did is not the focus of the discussion here, except for the fact that *its* background is also responsible for the extraordinary ambivalence— cultural, religious, ideological, psychological—which came to affect the twentieth-century German Jewish community—and then, too, the thought of Hannah Arendt, which is to be considered here. Moses Mendelssohn, the most prominent Jewish spokesman for the German Enlightenment,

140

answered the question of how the Jews of Germany could live up to ideals of emancipation and yet remain Jews, by endorsing the recommendation that they should attempt to be Jews in their homes and Germans in the street. But this was more easily said than done—as we recall now in the common parody of the statement which asserted that the Jews turned out to be Germans in their homes and Jews only in the street (that is, in the eyes of the Germans). This parody is something of an exaggeration, no doubt, but there was enough truth in it to attest to the continuing ambiguity between the public and the private lives of the Jews of Germany. To be sure, the strains between the public and the private, between civic life and private conscience, have been problems in the twentieth century not only for Judaism but for other religions as well—(and among Jews else-where, too, not only for those in Germany). But in an age when religious identity of every kind would be challenged, there was, for the Jew, the additional problem of discovering what public role he would be *allowed* even if he were willing to give up his private or religious commitments. The question of the relation between personal conscience or religious commitment, on the one hand, and a public or civic life, on the other, was, we shall see, a constant preoccupation of Hannah Arendt; it was also a factor in her conception of modern totalitarianism which was the basis for her view of what is referred to here as the "politics of evil."

There is perhaps no more pointed example of the conflicting alternatives between a public and a private self as they appeared to twentieth-century German Jewry than in the family history of one of its most intriguing and best-known offspring, Gershom Scholem, who, in his writings about Jewish mysticism, would substantially alter the understanding of Jewish religious history. As in the story recited in the Passover Hagaddah, there were in the Scholem household, located in middle-class Berlin at the turn of the century, four sons. Of these, Gershom was the youngest. Early in his life and almost entirely on his own initiative, Gershom identified himself with the Jewish tradition, undertook to study Hebrew and the classical texts, and became a Zionist. For such nonconformity, his father, when Gershom was about twenty, forced him to leave the family home and cut off relations with him (these relations were later, but only shakily, restored). Gershom emigrated to Palestine in 1923, took a position in the National Library and then in the newly founded Hebrew University—and

141

the rest of his story is known. Gershom's eldest brother had before this joined the family printing business and, in the process of becoming a man of affairs also became an ardent German patriot. After the Nazis took power, in 1938, he emigrated to Australia—but he would, thirty years later and even after everything that had occurred in the intervening years, *still* describe himself as a German nationalist. The next-to-eldest brother more or less accepted the values of the Scholem parents themselves: conservative politically and liberal with respect to Judaism, stopping just short of full assimilation. The third brother, Werner, who was closest in age to Gershom, chose to join the Communist party and was eventually elected to the Reichstag as a deputy of the Party. In his arguments with Gershom the Zionist, it was Werner's view that the so-called Jewish Question was, in fact, a human question—that the status of the Jews in Germany (indeed, of Jews any place in the world) was an issue not of maintaining Jewish identity, but of achieving universal social justice. This brother was killed by the Nazis in Buchenwald in 1940. Four brothers—four very different conceptions of Jewish identity and four different destinies—in the face of what had been, after all, a single and common starting point.

I would add to this brief family survey a reference to two other items that Gershom Scholem himself notes in his autobiography. The first of these is an incident that he relates. At the age of fourteen, he received the gift of a photograph of Theodore Herzl from his non- or (in the case of his father) anti-Zionist parents. There was for him, first, the oddity of this gift as it came to him from them, and there was, secondly, the occasion—it was his parents' Christmas gift to him. The second item is his report that, to the best of his knowledge, and despite his father's emphasis on the identity of German Jews as Germans and despite his father's standing in the business community which brought him many acquaintances in the sociable city of Berlin—never once had a non-Jew entered the family home. So much, one might say, for the hope that the Jews might appear to the *Germans* as Germans.

Hannah Arendt's family history, which began in Kant's city of Königsberg, was not as dramatic or as symptomatic as Scholem's—although, since the names of Hannah Arendt and Gershom Scholem have now been mentioned together, this brief parenthesis of social history should also be completed: after a sharp exchange of letters between them following the publication of Arendt's book on the Eichmann trial. Scholem, who had been a friend of Arendt's, never spoke to her again.

I mention these ancedotes instead of moving directly to discuss the "politics of evil" both for themselves and also for a purpose—and this is to suggest that Arendt's reflections on the modern history of evil involve much the same ambivalence (verging at times on inconsistency) that we find in the details of her history and in many of her writings but, especially, those that have Judaism and Zionism as their subjects. Arendt is, it seems to me, basically an ironical writer, continually asserting that what seems to be the case often turns out to be exactly its opposite, that even what appears to be the most monstrous evil may, in fact, be something else. As for many passionate ironists, this tendency often leaves both her and her readers, when we ask about her basic commitments, in a quandary. It is not unusual that we should find the life or biography of a philosopher embodied in his or her thinking—and, in many ways, Arendt seems, in her writing as well as in her life, to personify the history—in a sense, also the end—of German Jewry. She would never, *did never,* question or doubt her identification as a Jew.* But how to translate that identification into an *identity* was constantly weighted for her with ambiguities; these do not resolve themselves even now when we are in a position to reflect on her life and thought as a whole.

This same tendency to ambiguity and irony plays a central role in Arendt's discussion of what she claims to be the new form which evil assumes in the twentieth century, in the new explanations we find there of how evil comes to exist and of how it does its work. To be sure, in one form or other these issues have a long history in religion and philosophy as well as in everyday life—but we can, I believe, discover in Arendt's thinking a coherent and valuable response to such questions. The trail begins here about mid-point in her writings and then extends backward and forward to other of her books. The mid-point I refer to is her report

---

* We might recall here the statement by Rahel Varnhagen soon before her death, which Arendt quotes with great deliberation and emphasis at the beginning of her biography of Varnhagen: "The thing which all my life seemed to be the greatest shame, which was the misery and misfortune of my life—having been born a Jewess—this I should on no account now wish to have missed." In *Rahel Varnhagen,* trans. Richard and Clara Winston (New York, 1974), p. 3.

on the trial of Adolf Eichmann—*Eichmann in Jerusalem: A Report on the Banality of Evil*. Arendt's analysis of the Eichmann trial has usually been read and interpreted—and—criticized—as if it were quite independent of her other writings; but it is only by relating this book to those other writings that we can understand her position on the nature—and sometime "banality"—of evil. This does not mean that Arendt's conclusions on this issue are adequate or even that they are consistent—and critics have attacked her on both those counts. But even allowing for such criticism, her account sheds an unusual and valuable light on totalitarianism, a form of political organization which was, in her view, a unique phenomenon, an invention of the twentieth century and, finally, also, a new development in the history of evil. Even the term which she uses to designate that evil—its "banality"—has newly entered the language.

Arendt's report of the trial of Eichmann, a report which appeared in 1963, originally as a series of articles in the *New Yorker* and then, soon afterward, as a volume, became a center of controversy as soon as it was published, although it should also be recalled that the strongest reactions to the book were *not* directed at its provocative title. The main protests took issue with a less prominent theme—her discussion of the role, during the Holocaust, of the Jewish communal structures, in particular the Jewish councils or *Judenräte*. It was Arendt's contention that the Nazis were abetted in their design by these Jewish communal organizations—in part by specific decisions which the councils and their leaders made, in part by the very *existence* of the councils. By their decisions in response to Nazi dictates—Arendt claimed—the councils, in effect, collaborated with the Nazis; by their very existence, they encouraged passivity and the illusion of hope at a time when what should have been encouraged was precisely the opposite of these.

Arendt was not the first writer to make these charges, but she was undoubtedly the most influential one to have done so, and her accusation gained in emphasis by its appearance in connection with the trial of a man whose inculpation in the events of the Holocaust was undeniable. The reaction to Arendt's rather brief comments on this topic was proportionately harsh; and it seems clear now, in light of the evidence, that, in the charges she made, Arendt was guilty at least of oversimplification—for example, that what she characterized as the universal reaction of the Jewish communities to the Nazi threat was, in fact, far from uniform. But the inadequacy of her account on this point is less relevant for the moment than the fact that her position here was part of a more general view that she held of the "politics of evil"—a view which attempted to describe what happened to the individual and his moral character—and to communities—under the weight of totalitarianism. In order to see *this* development, however, we have to turn to the more central theme of Arendt's book on the Eichmann trial—that is, to her conception of the "banality of evil" as she applied that phrase to Eichmann and, by implication, to many others.

About this theme of her book, too, the reaction of Arendt's formulation was severe—and here, also, it seems that she invited this reaction. To describe the role of a central figure in the Holocaust as banal seems unavoidably to diminish both the enormity of what occurred in the Holocaust itself and the culpability of those responsible for it. Arendt did not, as she herself pointed out, agree with these implications—but she was obviously willing to risk them, and the reason for this was the unusual conception of evil that she located in the person and actions of Eichmann.

One thing which the trial in Jerusalem had made quite clear, in Arendt's opinion, was what Eichmann was *not*. If we ordinarily mean by evil the acts of a person who, like Iago in Shakespeare's *Othello,* moves at every turn to cause suffering and then, having succeeded, takes pleasure in that result, someone who commits himself to evil as a principle—this was not the Eichmann who was revealed at his trial, even on the strongest arguments of the prosecution, The charge that evil had been chosen knowingly, chosen for the sake of evil itself, simply did not match up with the acts of the man in the glass booth in Jerusalem, even after taking into account all of the evidence against him. Here was a man who repeatedly insisted that the scenes which he observed in his trips to the camps of the East were repugnant to him; who claimed—evidently with the expectation of being believed—that, notwithstanding the terrible history of which he had been part, he, "personally," had nothing against Jews. Here was a man who would cite Kant's Categorical Imperative to justify his own obedience to the order given for the Final Solution: If he had disobeyed those orders, so Eichmann's version of Kant went, every soldier would be justified in disobeying whatever orders he happened to object to.

There are undoubtedly various ways of understanding a person who had done what Eichmann had done (and what he freely admitted to having done) in organizing the deportation of hundreds of thousands of Jews but who would, on the other hand, express the views just mentioned. Arendt's conception of the banality of evil is one such judgment, although here, too, it is important to understand what she means by the phrase and what she does not mean by it. The term *banality* sometimes refers to what is common or commonplace—and readers who interpret the phrase in this way take it to mean that Eichmann had acted "commonly"—that is, not much differently from the way other people would have acted had they been in his place. This interpretation brings Arendt dangerously close to asserting that Eichmann's failings, even if we judge them as crimes, were, after all, only human—that there is, perhaps, a similar potential for evil in every human being and, thus, finally, that there was nothing unusual about Eichmann himself. And *this* conclusion, if it does not absolve Eichmann, certainly diminishes the weight of the charges against him.

But there is an alternate reading of "banality" which, it seems to me, comes closer to Arendt's intention—and which also underlies her conception of the politics of evil. If calling evil "banal" means that a person acts as he does because although as a human being he *might* have thought clearly about what he was doing but did not; that he only echoed disconnected ideas or ideals which he had taken over from others without understanding them; that he did not think enough about what he was doing to recognize what its consequences would be, or that the so-called principles on which he was choosing to act were self-contradictory; if, in other words, the evil-doer was a "hollow man," emptied of whatever it is that distinguishes human beings as human—*then* the result of this would be the banality, the sheer mechanical thoughtlessness, of the evildoer.

This, it seems to me, is, indeed, Arendt's judgment of Eichmann who could not, or at least would not, think about what he was doing. He was not, in these terms, irrational or mad—it was, rather, a matter of being nonrational, of looking human but not quite *being* human. The surest evidence of this for Arendt was the fact that Eichmann seemed unable to recognize a connection between himself and other human beings;* he

---

* See *Eichmann in Jerusalem: A Report on the Banality of Evil* (New York, 1977), p. 48.

could not put himself in the place of others, that act of moral imagination which is a condition for moral judgment of any kind. How else, Arendt argues, could someone see no inconsistency between sending hundreds of thousands of people to their deaths and continuing to believe that he had nothing "personal" against them? Arendt finds this banality epitomized— it is at this point in her book that she first introduces the phrase the "banality of evil"—in Eichmann's last words, uttered only a short time before he was to be hanged. Even at that hour, she emphasizes, he remained the captive of words he had heard but had not thought. In his speech, he praises Germany, the country he had served; Austria, his native land; and Argentina, the country which provided him with a refuge after the war, until he was seized there by the Israeli agents. He would, he says, with a lack of self-consciousness that verges on unconsciousness, "never forget them."

It seems to me that this is about as far as we can go in understanding what Arendt intended by her phrase, the "banality of evil"—although, again, saying this does not mean that no objections can be raised against the view itself. When Arendt asserts that Eichmann was "thoughtless," a "caricature," a "clown" (it is also to these characteristics that she attributes the "banality"), it seems unlikely that anyone reflecting on the Holocaust would ordinarily associate those terms with the world that Eichmann had inhabited. In speaking in this way of Eichmann, Arendt ignores certain important distinctions—and she also, at a deeper level, places unusual weight on the power of thinking or reason itself, as if the capacity to think would suffice, by itself, to prevent the occurrence of evil. Was it only because Eichmann did not know how to think that he did what he did? How much of evildoing even outside the Holocaust would that explain?

These last questions bring us closer to the "politics of evil" and, indeed, to the problem of evil more generally. Arendt's critics objected to her conception of the "banality of evil" because it seemed to diminish Eichmann's responsibility—and the same objection would apply to a view of evil as the product of thoughtlessness. In everyday life, if someone does not intend to do something, if a person acts accidentally or when he intends to do something else, if he acts without thinking—then we would ordinarily agree that his responsibility for what he does is diminished. At an extreme, for people who are insane or for young children, we excuse them for all responsibility whatever. The history of ethical thinking as a whole is, in fact, sharply divided between two contradictory views of the relation between knowledge and moral responsibility. On one side in this dispute we find a so-called rationalist view of ethics, according to which reason and knowledge are all-powerful. For ethical thinkers in this tradition—for example, Plato—no one never does evil knowingly or intentionally, no one ever *wants* to do wrong. If people knew that what they were doing was evil, this knowledge, by itself, would compel them to avoid it. Thus, when someone does wrong, he does it because he believes that what he is doing is good, not evil. He may be mistaken about that, of course, but then, too, he acts out of ignorance. And if someone acts out of ignorance, his responsibility is considerably diminished; at most, he is responsible for not knowing something he should have known, and this responsibility does not apply in every case.

This may seem a very mild explanation of the phenomenon of evil—as can be seen from the contrasting view which is vividly represented in the Western religious traditions, in a radical form in Christianity and, somewhat more moderately, in Judaism. Here the claim is made that it is, indeed, possible to know something to be wrong and to do it anyway (this, it has been argued, is precisely the capacity which Adam and Eve acquired by their first disobedience). Knowledge by itself, on these accounts, does not avert evildoing, since the *will* to do evil is also a factor. Thus, ignorance may *sometimes* explain why wrongs are done, but not always—and when we find that someone who does wrong knew what he was doing—or if he didn't know, that he *should* have known—he is, to that extent, responsible both for what he did and for its consequences.

It seems clear that Arendt's view of Eichmann and the banality of evil is committed to the first of these two alternatives: Eichmann, in her judgment, simply did not think, perhaps he did not even have the capacity to think, about what he was doing—and the implications of her stress on this is that if *he had* thought about it he would have acted differently, or at least that whatever evil he did would not have been banal. Even holding this, however, believing that in some sense Eichmann did not know what he was doing, Arendt holds that Eichmann should have been punished as he was, concluding finally that there was no alternative.

Now it might be objected that there is an inconsistency here—that Arendt's explanation of why Eichmann did what he did contradicts the judgment that she passes on him. It is not clear to me how Arendt would have responded to this criticism; but of more basic importance in any event, it seems to me, is the fact that Arendt's ambiguous judgment of Eichmann is, itself, part of a larger view of the politics of evil that Arendt had begun to develop long before the Eichmann trial. Seen against *that* background, in fact, Eichmann appears as an example of a new *kind* of evildoer, one which comes into existence with twentieth-century totalitarianism. For with that development, Arendt claims, we discover a new stage in the moral history of mankind: something changes in the character of evil, for its agents and even for its victims. Thus, her writings that describe this change also become pertinent to the attempt to understand, or, at least, represent, Eichmann.

In 1951, Arendt published what for many of her readers remains her most important book, *The Origins of Totalitarianism*. It was her most sustained response to the phenomenon of Nazism which had been brought to an abrupt end only a few years before, and which before that had radically disrupted Arendt's own life. In 1933, she left Germany for France; she was able to find work there mainly on behalf of various Jewish organizations, but after the Nazi invasion of France she was briefly in an internment camp. At the beginning of 1941, she came to the United States, where she would live for the rest of her life, and where she soon began work on *The Origins of Totalitarianism*. Characteristically, her analysis of Nazism attempted to place that phenomenon in the context of a broader historical background, first by relating it to the history of anti-Semitism, and then by considering it as only one instance of the totalitarianism which was, for her, an innovation of the twentieth-century. She recognized, of course, that there had been dictatorial and repressive governments before this century, and that there had also been many instances of cruelty by individuals acting in the name of governments. What was distinctive for her about totalitarianism, which was epitomized for her in the concentration camps of the Nazis (and, also, she added, in the Russian Gulag), was one feature in particular: that here, for the first time, appeared an idea of evil which called for the extinction of man as an individual. Other forms of repression had been intended to intimidate people, to convert them to other doctrines or beliefs or even to destroy them. But in totalitarianism, according to Arendt, we find for the first time an *ideal* that the individual was to be eliminated as an individual: he was to become only an appendage, subordinate to a larger historical purpose. "Totalitarianism," she writes, "strives not toward despotic rule over men, but toward a system in which men are superfluous." That this "superfluity of man," the elimination of the individual person should be held as a principle—or, even, for that matter, as a possibility—was, in Arendt's view, something that even the extreme instances of barbarism in the past had not discovered. Moreover, this principle affects everyone caught up in the net of totalitarianism, its perpetrators as well as its victims. It may seem odd to consider the agents of totalitarianism under the same heading as we do its victims, but Arendt was prepared to go this far as well: in totalitarianism, as in many other systems of evil, the perpetrator himself also was affected, if not in the same *terms,* equally fundamentally. At its extreme, totalitarianism obliterates individual freedom and reason on both sides: the superfluity of man, in other words, becomes a general principle, encompassing the system as a whole and everyone caught up by it.*

It is to this aspect of totalitarianism—which comes into existence only as recent means of social organization and recent means of technology make it possible—that my phrase, the "politics of evil," refers. For what Arendt implies here is not just that one form of political expression represents evil to a degree beyond the capacity of any single system *or* individual; it is, in effect, the epitome of evil. The most radical expression of evil, in other words, is political and not simply moral (meaning by the latter, the decisions or acts of an individual like Iago or even Satan)—and we can understand how Arendt reaches this conclusion. Before the twentieth century, it was reasonable to assume that the control of individual conscience or freedom rested finally, for better *or* for worse, in the hands of individuals acting on their own. But for totalitarianism as a system, evil is intrinsic, not something separately decided on; as a system, furthermore, it is more effective in accomplishing the goals of evil than any individual decisions or acts could be, no matter now monstrous. Evil

---

* *The Origins of Totalitarianism* (New York, 1966), pp. 456–457.

which traditionally has been associated with individual decisions and acts, turns out, in the lesson taught by the twentieth century, to be political rather than moral.

How, then, do we come back from the politics of evil to the banality of evil? But remember again Arendt's characterization of Eichmann's banality—for we see him now as exemplifying what she has described as the effects of totalitarianism. Eichmann, who was himself the *agent* of totalitarianism, abetting the work of the death camps which were its fullest expression, was also an expression or symptom, in some perverse sense also a victim, of that political form. He was, himself, superfluous as a human being, retaining the appearance of a person, but lacking the capacity for freedom and reason that were, for Arendt, essential to the definition of any such being. Arendt goes so far as to claim that totalitarianism had produced a change not only in how people acted toward each other, but in human nature itself, in what man was. This was an extreme claim which has in turn itself been disputed by her critics—but it is by understanding its extremity that we now also understand her account of Eichmann and the banality of evil.

To be sure, the fact that the account I have given finds connections among quite separate parts of Arendt's thinking does not mean that those connections (even if the formulation here were accepted) are not also open to question. When Arendt describes the phenomenon of Nazism simply as an instance of totalitarianism in general, or when she equates the Nazi death camps with the Russian Gulag—it may well seem that she overlooks important differences. And, again, the question arises of whether twentieth-century totalitarianism is, indeed, the innovation that she says it is, either in the history of politics or in the history of evil: it has been argued, on the other side, that genocide itself is not peculiar to the twentieth century. There remain, finally, the questions which her account of totalitarianism raises about the issue of guilt and responsibility. If Eichmann acted as he did because of the expression of totalitarianism as a political form, in what sense was he—or anyone else—responsible for what was done? And how does one explain the fact that some Germans avoided, or in a few cases even resisted, being caught up in the killing operations of the Nazis?

These are all compelling questions, and it is not clear to me how Arendt would have answered them or, indeed, if she could answer them. But there is at least one side of her account which Arendt extends consistently and constantly—and this is the connection that she emphasizes between politics and the public life, on the one hand, and the moral life of the individual, on the other. It is not surprising, in fact, that, for Arendt, politics should engender the most extreme form of evil—for, at the other end of the spectrum, it is politics that makes goodness possible in the first place. This discussion began with certain references to the distinction between their public and their private lives that generations of German Jews had taken as an ideal. Arendt did not deny that there could or should be differences—a space—between these two domains, but it was much more important for her that there should be a basic consistency between them, with the public life assuring the means that make the private life of judgment and thought possible. The reason why, in her view, the Enlightenment of the eighteenth century failed, notwithstanding its high-minded promises of the rights and dignity of man, was the same reason that the Enlightenment also came to be inculpated in the origins of totalitarianism: the political structures required to assure those rights had never been set up. The political structures which *had* evolved could not guarantee to minorities the rights that the idealistic rhetoric had spoken about—because the structure did not allow minorities to speak in their own voice.

In this sense, although Arendt did not apply the term to herself, she was, in contemporary terms, a conservative. It was, for her, only the individual communal unit or council, even the much maligned nation—in any event, a unit that was the expression of a particular not a universal voice—that would assure the rights of particular citizens and their particular interests. On this basis, when she considered the question of Zionism, Arendt argued for the need, and then for the legitimacy, of the state of Israel. The Jews had lived, she contended, as a "Pariah" people, as outcasts. The basic character of their existence in Europe was what she called Jewish "worldlessness," a condition in which they had no public life—or at least no *assurance* of such a life. And for these liabilities, the state of Israel was a solution—although, as history was to turn out, her conception of the political structures and policies that Israel *should* adopt was sharply at odds with the directions in which Israel went. From the same arguments used to endorse a balance between the private and the

public life, moreover, came her opposition to the idea of a world government which would, in her view, overpower the private domain; it would
be, she wrote, "the worst tyranny imaginable."* If governments did not
have limits, they would be unwilling to express the particular interests of
the diverse groups of their citizens.

Obviously, these views of Arendt's are open to dispute. But however
we judge them in themselves, one conclusion which seems undeniable
follows from them collectively—and this is her claim for the necessary
relation between political structures and the moral life of the individual.
In some sense, to be sure, this relation is obvious: *of course,* our social
or political surroundings have consequences for what we are, or do, as
individuals. And, of course, the domain of private belief or conscience
cannot simply be replaced by the public one. But Arendt's point goes
deeper than these, as it attempts to show what the connections between
the two are, how they work. Even here, of course, there is room for
disagreement—as is also, and more emphatically, true for her study of
Eichmann. But notwithstanding such possibilities, it is worth remarking
that Arendt remains one of only a very few writers willing even to try to
characterize evil in the form that it took during the Holocaust. There have
been studies and biographies aplenty of Nazi leaders, and there have been
attempts, on the other side, to analyze figures in the Holocaust who were
morally exemplary. But few studies other than hers have attempted to
analyze the events of the Holocaust as the evil which appears there.

Thus, notwithstanding the criticism that has been directed against other
aspects of Arendt's work, her conception of the relation between politics
and the life of the individual, between the public domain and private
conscience, and, eventually between good and evil, remains. She continually revised her position on the details of these relations; in her later
writings, the balance she had seen between the public and the private
domains shifted much more strongly in the direction of the private (her
last book, still being written when she died in 1975, was titled *The Life
of the Mind*). But one might think of this shift, too, as only another swing
of the pendulum, not as an attempt to settle her last word on the subject.
Arendt, I have suggested, was more given to ambivalence or irony than

---

* *Lectures on Kant's Political Philosophy* (Chicago, 1982), 44.

to last words, anyway. This was, itself, her most basic commitment: that, for anyone who thought independently, there *would* always be another word to be said. This does not mean that it is impossible to judge between good and evil—and, indeed, I have been suggesting that it is here, in her account of totalitarianism and the politics of evil, that Arendt's contribution to that judgment developed. Her account of the politics of evil reflected the conflict between the private and public domains which had affected her own life as it did the lives of almost every European Jew in the first half of the twentieth century. It hardly needs to be pointed out that the same conflict, in only slightly different terms, continues in the present as well.

18

Language and Genocide

The explanation of a historical event inevitably bears the mark of artifice. If it did not omit or compress, it would be as extensive as the events it was intended to explain and would be no more coherent than they were individually. To be sure, it is not only because of the complexity of historical connections in general that even the most sustained attempts to identify the causes of the Nazi genocide against the Jews seem inadequate. The difficulties here add the extraordinary character of that occurrence to the unusual status of evil itself, which even in less extreme appearances seem always to leave a remainder after the apparent social, economic, or psychological factors have been named. Beyond these intrinsic constraints, moreover, we recognize the scale on which the Nazi genocide was set—crossing the boundaries of continents, involving as victims, agents, and bystanders scores of nations, tens of millions of people. Accounts of an event of these magnitudes must be hard put even to distinguish between causes and effects, let alone to determine the exact points at which they met; it would be a considerable accomplishment, in fact, to establish a bare chronicle of the event—what *happened,* and this indeed remains the single most important task of all writing about that event.

Thus, too, the assertion which will be made here of a connection between language and the Nazi genocide may seem hardly to move beyond the claim that language was at once a victim of the genocide and one agent of many among its causes. But acknowledgment of even the connection itself is significant; the violence done to language in the genocide—in a special sense, to the German language, in a larger sense, to language as such—provides a distinctive representation of what the intention to exterminate the Jews required of its perpetrators in the way of will and of artifice; it discloses how deeply set the design of genocide was and how fully developed a worldview it became. The Nazi genocide, seen from the perspective of language, is unusual in another respect as well—

since from this perspective, the victims are seen to include those who shaped or only used the language in addition to those against whom the work of genocide was directed. The distortion of language is in this sense a more generalized violation than others that have more obviously terrible consequences and in which the distinction between agents and victims is explicit and constant. To escape the consequences of language, for worse or for better, would require an impossible step outside history for its speakers or writers no less than for its audience—and whatever else we discover about the Nazi genocide, the evidence is only too clear of its place *within* history, as motivated and embodied in historical cause as well as in effect.

The background to this claim is broader than the specific evidence of the role of language in the Nazi genocide. The existence of a causal relation between language and history, between linguistic practice and events in the social context, would be disputed only on the view of language as a neutral and transparent medium, perhaps following certain formal rules of development but even then serving as an incidental means for the prior and more "real" intentions of its speakers or writers. On this view, the capacity of language is independent of its objects; thus the moral character of the events of which language provides a representation is of no consequence for the detail of syntax and vocabulary on the basis of which the representation is formulated. In the terms made current by de Saussure, the "signifier" and the "signified" which constitute the linguistic transaction are arbitrarily related to each other—and also, beyond that, to the historical events which they are then, however mysteriously, understood to denote. On this view, neither natural nor historical causality influences the structure or stylistic patterns of language; nor, conversely, do the forms of language, whether in actual usage or in formal structure, reflect in any significant way what is said by their means. *What* is said is thus held to be independent of *how* it is said; the same "thing" can be expressed in quite different ways and across what appear as quite different linguistic structures. It is linguistic content that has consequences—the descriptions or commands that are given, the purposes that are announced and the evidence which is credited—but not, in any event, the variations in form of their expressions.

The narrowness of this view of language would be demonstrable even without the unusual evidence provided by the linguistic embodiment of the intentions directing the Nazi genocide. Testimony comes from many different sources of the history of language as "real" history, evolving in direct relation to features of the historical and social context. Those features extend from the constraints imposed by human physiology to the effects of specific technological developments like the alphabet or the printing press—and then also, to the consequences of radical political change that may affect not only specific linguistic usage but the concept of language as such. So de Maistre would write that "every individual or national degradation is immediately heralded by a strictly proportional degradation in the language itself"—and his words here, one infers, bear not only on "degradation" but, more generally, on all significant change.

The relation between linguistic practice and the causes that affect it, moreover, includes among those causes the content of specific linguistic expressions as well as the social history external to language. Thus, a central issue in the history of literature has focused on the problem of genres—the relation between literary forms or means, on the one hand, and the content of the texts that have those forms, on the other. The difficulty that becomes evident from such analysis of sustaining a sharp distinction between form and content would itself suggest their interrelation, and this conclusion is further supported as instances of supposedly formal stylistic analysis revert, as they constantly do, to the question of content: what the literary text is "about" or "of." As the corporate forms of expression—art, legal institutions, religious practice—reflect varieties of purpose and moral agency at their origins, moreover, it is hardly surprising that this should also be the case for language which is another such form—one, in fact, on which the others depend. Indeed, as soon as discourse is conceived as a means of agency on the part of a speaker, this connection is made: *some* understanding of origin and purpose becomes associated with meaning; as historical, those sources then affect the shape of expression.

On these general grounds, it is predictable that linguistic developments which occurred at the time of the Nazi genocide would disclose features resembling those of the process of genocide itself; it would be difficult to understand how the latter might occur without corresponding changes in the language. The evidence that there was such a connection is the basis

157

of the discussion here—a connection which extends, moreover, to the *idea* of language as well as to specific patterns of usage. As individual features of language—syntax, grammar, figures of speech—come to be viewed in the Nazi vocabulary as mere instruments, subordinated in rhetoric or art or theoretical discourse to political ends, so in the role of language applied to the work of genocide, language as a whole is conceived as an instrument, also subordinated to ends determined independently of it. Language is in this process detached from history and nature and finally also from moral judgment—a means only by which certain intentions, themselves independently defined and allegedly trans-linguistic, are to be implemented. It thus takes on the character of impersonal technique, to be applied to whatever ends its agents independently decide on and reflecting only as much of those ends as the agents determine that it should. Language, in other words, becomes entirely contrivance, mute with respect to its own voice, detached from any sense of its own origins or purposes.

This conception of language differs markedly from another and more traditional view according to which language is historically bound—caused by and expressive of the agent who speaks or writes it. On these terms, language is linked intrinsically to thought and social practice, reflecting or representing its agents and their purposes as well as the objects to which it refers. To be sure, extreme versions of the latter view—where a particular language was identified first with nature with a source of self-legitimating authority (civil or religious)—could be as dogmatic in their consequences as the opposed claim that there are no such connections; they were no less common, moreover, than were the visions of a "universal," artificial language such as that proposed by Leibniz. What was historically decisive in the relation between genocide and language, however, was the displacement at the levels of both concept and practice of the view of language as a form of disclosure and expression. In that displacement, we find the willed recreation of language entirely as an instrument or means, together with the condition presupposed by that change: the claim by political authority to authority also over social memory and history; the reconstruction of language as entirely ideological and thus as independent of facts, on the one hand, and of human agency, on the other; the assertion of political power to fill the space which is left by the denial to language of all authority of its own.

These summary comments about the general relation between language and history do not depend only on the consequences for language of the Nazi genocide against the Jews or even, at a more general level than that, on the technological and totalitarian character of the Nazi state which were conditions, and undoubtedly necessary conditions, of that genocide. It is evident, moreover, that aspects of what is alleged here to characterize the language of the Nazis can be found in other linguistic usage as well, certainly as a consequence of the Nazis' own precedent, but in some measure also prior to it. Yet as in other respects the Nazi by what they did defined paradigmatically the act of genocide, so too, through their explicit and methodical elaboration of that act—the *constancy* of their intentions—they provide an extraordinary view of the role that language both had and suffered in the phenomenon of genocide.*

One does not have to look for a significant instance of such usage beyond the term by which the Nazis chose to designate their genocidal war against the Jews—that is, the "Endlösung" or "Final Solution," which after the Wannsee Conference of 20 January, 1942 was adopted by Nazi officialdom as the code-word meant at once to disguise and to refer to that plan of extermination. In this term appear the characteristic features of a complex inversion of language—a linguistic equivalent of the very phenomenon to which the term itself refers; in it, we also see the form of the general turn that the language of genocide was to take.

It is well to understand that *Endlösung* had a history prior to its adoption by the Nazis, not so much as a term of general usage (although it was so used, although infrequently) as in the sense that other terms, close in meaning, had been "tried out" before the choice of Endlösung itself was

---

* Among the accounts given of the Nazi use of language, see especially Nachman Blumenthal, "On the Nazi Vocabulary," *Yad Vashen Studies* 1 (1957), 49–66; and "From the Nazi Vocabulary," 6 (1967), 69–82; Gordon A. Craig, *The Germans* (New York; 1982), 323–325; Shaul Esh, "Words and Their Meanings: Twenty-Five Examples of the Nazi-Idiom," *Yad Vashem Studies* 5 (1963), 133–167; Jean Pierre Faye, *Languages totalitaires* (Paris; 1972); Henry Friedlander, "The Manipulation of Language," in *The Holocaust: Ideology, Bureaucracy, and Genocide* (Millwood, N.Y., 1980), 103–114; Rolf Hochuth, "Als Nachwort ein Blick auf Wörter," in *Die Hebamme* (Reinbek; 1971), pp. 287–302; Eugen Seidel and Ingeborg Seidel, *Sprachwandel im Dritten Reich: Ein critisches Untersuchung faschischten Einflusse* (Halle; 1961); George Steiner, *Language and Silence* (New York; 1974), pp. 95–109.

made. So, there is reference to *Endziel* ("final goal") in Heydrich's order of 21 September 1934 to the Einsatzgruppen ("specially commissioned groups"); to *Gesamtlösung* ("total solution"), by Göring in his directive to Heydrich of 31 July 1941 (Göring in this same statement *also* uses "Endlösung"); and to the *Endgültige Lösung* ("conclusive solution") in a statement by Himmler concerning the "gypsy question" (8 December 1939). We have mainly to speculate about the process by which these alternatives came to be rejected in favor of "Endlösung" (for which Eichmann, probably on the basis of the Wannsee Conference, was to claim pride of authorship)—although one reason might well be that the latter term avoids possible ambiguities in the others: *Ziel* ("goal") as something that may or may not be within reach; *gesamt* ("total" or "collective") referring to all the parts of a problem at a given time but not necessarily to settling the problem once and for all.*

In any event, it seems evident that the Wannsee Conference at which the Endlösung was ratified in name and intention took for granted that term's implication of *other* "solutions" which had been proposed to the same "problem" or "question" as the one addressed at the conference, but that were not, by contrast, "final." It was not the Nazis, moreover, who initiated the use of the complementary terms—"question," or "problem," on the one hand, and "solution," on the other—in connection with discussions of the status of the Jews. The "Jewish Question" to which various solutions or answers *would* be sought and posed was in fact a conventional locution, used by non-Jewish—and anti-Jewish—writers, but also by Jewish and philo-Jewish writers, however differently from the former the latter understood the "question" or "problem" that was being raised.*

The first part of the agglutinative noun "Endlösung" as applied by the Nazis to the "Jewish Question" does, of course, also refer to the prior efforts of the Nazis themselves—the earlier and "less-than-final" solu-

---

*Göring was to offer a version of this distinction in his own defense at Nuremberg. See Gerald Reitlinger, *The Final Solution* (South Brunswick, N.J., 1968), p. 85.

*Perhaps the best-known use of hte term is in Marx's *Zur Judenfrage* (1844), but see also, for examples: Ahad Ha'am, "Medinat Ha-Yehudim Ve'Tsa-rat-Ha-Yehudim" ("The Jewish State and the Jewish Problem") (1897); Theodore Herzl, *Der Judenstaat, Versuch einer modernen Lösung der Judenfrage* (1896); Louis Brandeis, "The Jewish Problem and How to Solve It" (1915).

tions which the Nazis had been proposing virtually from the moment they came to power in 1933. Those efforts included the sequence of racial legislation epitomized by the Nuremberg Laws of 1935 which, by imposing a combination of economic and social restrictions, had as their principal purpose the confiscation of property and the coercion of Jewish emigration from Germany—a policy which persisted with some variations until the edict of 23 October 1941 prohibiting Jewish emigration. (This policy included the scheme for resettling the Jews in Madagascar, a plan which never came close to implementation but was the occasion of speculation between 1938 and 1940, and was certainly consistent with the policy of forced emigration—mentioned, among others, in statements by Göring, 12 November 1938, by Hans Frank in January 1940, and in February 1941 by Hitler himself.)* Proposals such as this, directed in common to the goal of a "Judenrein" Germany, were not "final solutions" for reasons that are only too evident. These proposals, moreover, had become increasingly problematic for the Nazis by the time of the Wannsee Conference, in part because the Nazis were encouraged by the lack of resistance to their earlier, less radical policies, but also because of the results of their military conquests. The partition of Poland between Germany and Russia on 28 September 1939 had itself brought almost two million Jews under Nazi control—and such developments afforded new temptation and new opportunity, including of course, the possibility that whatever the Nazis might now think of doing to the Jews could now be done farther from the sight of the West (indeed, farther from the sight of the Germans themselves) and with the aid of native populations whom the Einsatzgruppen discovered immediately after the invasion of Russia often to be willing collaborators. It was, then, in this context that the Endlosung was proposed—to solve the now larger "Jewish Question" in a plan of extermination that was to include *all* the Jews of Europe, those of Great Britain and of the neutral countries, Sweden and Switzerland, in addition to those in countries over which the Nazis already held power.*

---

* See Raul Hilberg, *The Destruction of the European Jews,* abridged edition (New York; 1985), pp. 154–161; also Leni Yachil, *The Holocaust: The Fate of European Jewry, 1932–1945* (Hebrew) (Tel-Aviv; 1987), pp. 358–360.

* Such plans were not matters only of fantasy. They were explicitly referred to in the protocol of the Wannsee Conference, and indeed Germany had at the end of June 1940

The superficial intelligibility from the point of view of the Nazis that is in this way supplied by the historical background of the term *Endlösung* joins the persuasive connotation of the term itself. For viewed out of context, in its dictionary meaning, Endlösung may seem even more benign a concept than its partial root, *Lösung*. Solutions are responses to problems which, by definition, are troublesome, hindering, things which *should* be overcome or solved. The latter also carry with them, in fact, the implied possibility of solution: to acknowledge something *as* a problem suggests also that it is capable of being solved. Thus, phrases such as "The Jewish Question" or "The Jewish Problem," even in formulations well disposed toward the "question," anticipate responses in the form of "solutions." Given the reasonable corollary, moreover, that if a problem is to be solved, it is best solved once and for all, an "Endlösung" is desirable in a way that provisional or incomplete solutions are not. Out of its historical context, then, the prospect of a "Final Solution" offers a welcome convergence of discursive and affective content: problems are meant to be solved—and the more fully or finally, the better.

And yet, of course, in the Nazi vocabulary *Endlösung* stands for the extermination of a people—not their deportation or their enslavement (although these also, as it happened), but their annihilation; this is the literal act to which the opposed connotation of the term was joined in the Nazi vocabulary. The blatant disparity between the normal connotation of the word, on the one hand, and its reference in that vocabulary, on the other, amounts to what in the usual conventions of linguistic meaning or social practice would be seen as a contradiction. Moreover, the fact that the Nazis themselves took the trouble to develop a set of "speech rules" explicitly intended to conceal literal meaning—among which the rule for the use of *Endlösung* occupied an important place*—suggests that they

---

occupied England's Channel Islands. Soon after that, legislation followed requiring the registration of the few Jews who lived on Jersey and Guernsey, and the sale of Jewish businesses to non-Jews; almost all the Jews identified were subsequently deported to concentration camps on the Continent. (A concentration camp was also constructed on Alderney; a number of Jews who had been transported from the Continent were killed there.) See Charles Cruickshank, *The German Occupation of the Channel Islands* (Channel Islands, 1975.

* These included limitations on its use altogether. So, Martin Bormann writes "on instructions from the Fuhrer" (11 July 1943) that there is henceforth to be "no public reference" to the Final Solution (Gesamtlösung). (See Yitzhak Arad et. al., *Documents from the Holocaust*

were themselves well aware of this tension. It must not be supposed, moreover, that the use of speech rules or a code was intended entirely or only for an external audience, that the Nazis among themselves were ready to speak openly—i.e., literally—of what the code concealed. For there is substantial evidence that the use of *Endlösung* (and of some, although not all, of the other terms to be discussed) was meant also in internal use to disguise or misrepresent something which it would have been dangerous or morally wrong to address more directly. This was so intrinsic a feature of the term that its own use was severely restricted: the code word itself was for limited circulation. Like other attempts at concealment by the Nazis which lead naturally to the question of *why* they sought to conceal it, speech rules provide important evidence of what the act of genocide represented in terms of Nazi beliefs—what, beyond what they *did*, they *thought* they were doing.

In selecting and using the term *Endlösung*, in any event, the Nazis were attempting to add to the referential force of the word elements that go well beyond the purposes of reference. What results from this process is a term that has been "figured" or "turned" much in the way that figurative language of any kind originates, reflecting, as such usage characteristically does, the intention to make a word mean more than it would in its literal appearance. There are, of course, various ways in which figurative discourse adds to the meaning of words, and it may seem perverse to suggest that an understanding of these literary means will be informative about a word with the extraordinary history—much more immediately social and political, after all, than literary—that *Endlösung* has had. Yet the probability that the turns of language reflect or display the turns of history is too evident to be ignored. Beyond the issue of this particular example, moreover, is a general question of the relation between "normal" and "abnormal" discourse, and then of the historical status of language as such; it is an instance again—as for the act of genocide more generally—where extremity serves as a proof or test of the ordinary.

Considered, then, against the background of conventional figures of speech, "Endlösung" may seem to have been intended as ironical, implying, as irony characteristically does, the opposite or at least a reversal of

(Jersusalem, 1981), p. 324. ("It may however be mentioned," Bormann's order concludes, that the Jews are taken in groups for appropriate labor purposes.")

what it superficially affirms: it denotes a solution to a problem by proposing the destruction of the problem. On this account, the term would be a
form of gallows humor, initiated from the point of view of the builder of
the gallows rather than that of the victim—a joke meant to be added to
the larger aggression.* But both internal and external evidence suggest
that it is not irony that is intended by the Nazi choice of the term, not
even the less pointed equivocation we find in *Endlösung* as we recognize
through it that not only the problem "to be solved" but also the *solutions*
to the problem would have come to an end; it would also, after all, be
the *last* solution. The purpose of the Nazi speech rules, however, was to
avoid calling attention to themselves and to their applications; this policy
was evident in the guarded references allowed even to the code words
themselves. Furthermore, there is at least one more general reason for
doubting that the Nazi purpose here was ironic. The characteristic feature
in irony of "double-vision," of language reiterating itself with a difference—and with a negation at that, to be supplied by the reader—makes
irony an unlikely feature of totalitarian discourse at any time. In this role,
irony underscores the possibility of nonliteral meaning and impels the
reader beyond the apparent text (thus also beyond censorship)—both of
these affording to both the writer and the reader a measure of freedom
that would undoubtedly be seen by totalitarianism as subversive.

In addition to such prima facie evidence, moreover, nothing in the
appearances of *Endlösung* in Nazi documents hints at an intention to undermine its surface meaning. It is rather the literal denotation, the deliberate assertion that through it the Jewish "problem" will be solved once
and for all, that is intended; and although for most instances of figurative
language (metaphor, for example) the absence of apparent intention from
the figure itself may be irrelevant or even an advantage, this is not the
case for irony. A statement or term which is read as metaphorical will
never have a meaning simply contradictory to the meaning of the same
statement or term read literally or nonmetaphorically. Irony alone has that

---

*Hilberg cites a counterpart to the Nazi vocabulary in that of the victims—for example,
the designation in Auschwitz of the crematorium as "the bakery"; see *The Destruction of
the European Jews* (New York, 1985), pp. 1041–1042. But what might be irony from the
point of view of the victim is something quite different in the Nazi vocabulary. (A more
recent example: a "hitler" has become the colloquial name of Israeli Hebrew for a household
device that kills or drives away flies by the fumes it gives off.)

feature, and for it intention is crucial. There is no irony that does not itself disclose the will responsible for it; still less could there be irony that is altogether unwilled.

For the audience who were "in" on the secret of the Nazi language rules, the term *Endlösung* denoted the extermination of the Jews—although even for them, it was meant at once to affirm and to obscure the referent: to focus attention on the goal and thus to draw attention away from the means. To the German public or the public outside Germany, as they might encounter the term and half know, half not know what it referred to, it would, on one level in any event, have the benign connotation of designating something that ought to be done—tautologically, the resolution of a problem that should be overcome *because* it was a problem, with the accompanying concealment that abstraction—"solution"—always provides when it replaces the name or image of a concrete act— "extermination." No space remains for irony at either end of this combination of contradictory meanings.

The question thus persists: if "Endlösung" is not irony, what figure or trope of speech is it? For the term is evidently contrived, turned, figurative in *some* way; certainly it is not innocent or straightforward, not matter-of-fact or literal in its overall force, despite—more accurately, because of—the evident intention which *is* part of it that it should be *understood* literally. This apparently academic question about figurative discourse is not at all academic in its results. For among the four classical literary figures under which varieties of the linguistic turn are often subsumed, irony has already been ruled out— and none of the other three provides a more adequate account: not metaphor (the "solution" is meant literally as a solution: tenor and vehicle are one); not metonymy (as "final," the solution is not a part substituted for a whole); not synechdoche (again, Endlösung is a *denial* of the part-whole relation). Related or similar objections block the appeal to more restricted figures of speech. The suggestion often made that "Endlösung" is an instance of euphemism, for example, although superficially plausible, is no more adequate than would be the suggestion that it is hyperbole. To refer to someone as having "gone to sleep" rather than as having died is to intend a euphemism based on a metaphor. The literal and the euphemistic versions agree at least that the person referred to is motionless and unconscious; the euphemistic connotation of sleep adds the comforting possibility of peace-fulness and perhaps of a later awakening. But when the description of an act has a connotation added to it that *revises* it, turning it not aside but into its opposite, we may reasonably conclude that the linguistic turn taken is not euphemism but a different figure altogether.

It seems hardly too much to claim here, in fact, that with "Endlösung" (and the related terms mentioned below), the language of genocide has contrived a distinctive literary figure. The characteristics of this figure are that the denotation of the term, although logically consistent with it (in principle, *any* act might be called a solution) substantively contradicts it; that the term itself is abstract and general but designates an event or object that is concrete and specific; and that the figurative term is meant to draw attention away from both this change and from the individual aspects of its referent, thus concealing what is denoted (and attempting to conceal the fact of concealment as well). The figure of speech thus consti-tuted diverges in each of these three respects from the common purpose of figurative language, which is at once to bring into focus—to "figure"—certain concrete aspects of the referent *and* to call attention to itself (and to itself as figurative).

I propose, quite simply, to call this new figure by an old name, one which more usually would not be associated with *figures* of speech at all—that is, the lie.* The reasons for invoking this term should, however, be clear: as the person who is a liar knowingly affirms what is false, so here a linguistic expression affirms what *it* "knows" to be false. Moral violation thus takes on the guise of literary form. Admittedly, one can anticipate objections to this (or any) claim for a linguistic version of ethical principle. For one thing, figurative language is usually viewed as distinguishable from the speaker's own—extra-linguistic—purposes, which can be understood literally and as the proper object of moral judg-ment. Thus speakers or writers may use hyperbole and other literary figures for the *purpose* of lying but still avoid lying *within* those figures: it is the action which the words serve that is in these cases subject to moral assessment. Moreover, when figurative language associated with

---

* See for an anticipation of this conception of the linguistic lie, Harold Weinrich, *Lin-guistik de Lüge* (Heidelberg, 966), pp. 34–41; see Bertholt Brecht, "Fünf Schwierigkeiten beim Schreiben der Wahrheit," (Frankfurt, 1948).

poetry or fictional discourse is meant to be ornamental, an imaginative heightening of aspects or objects which would otherwise have only a nonfigurative, "literal" existence, this is not usually judged to be a lie or instance of deception. "Achilles is a lion" is not *intended* to be understood literally; if it were, the statement would be a lie as well as false. On the other hand, the distinction between figurative and moral discourse seems inadequate for understanding the figurative terms defined by the Nazi speech rules: their moral quality (morally problematic, that is) is so fundamental as to be part of the expression itself, to be engaged in the *manner* of speaking. A person who denies having done something he knowingly did is lying—but it is not the language that then does the lying, it is the speaker. By contrast, calling genocide a "final solution" turns the phrase itself into a lie, in the same sense that the representation of Achilles as a "lion" discloses the latter term to be a metaphor for anyone who otherwise understands the literal denotation of those two terms. The figurative lie links two contradictory literal references; it also attempts, in asserting the connection, both to deny the contradiction and to conceal the denial. (Oxymoron, although it includes the former feature, that of the contradiction, does not have the latter.) To be sure, a speaker or writer who employs the figure of the lie will often, perhaps even necessarily, be lying also in the moral sense: language does not, after all, speak itself. But there is still the distinction to be made between the language and its user; as the tropes or figures of speech belong to the language apart from any individual application, so now does the figure of the lie.

To focus discussion of the language of genocide on the term by which the Nazis designated the act of genocide itself is to cite only one example of many possible ones; there is, in fact, a general "vocabulary" that provides much broader evidence of the role of the figurative lie. An important example among these is the lengthy list of words substituted in the Nazi vocabulary for "killing" or "execution." *Sonderbehandlung* ("special treatment") comes closest among these terms to repeating the linguistic conditions mentioned in connection with "Endlösung,"* but

---

* The first use of "Sonderbehandlung" in this sense is attributed to Heydrich in a letter of 20 September 1939—directed against Germans rather than Jews. See Joseph Wulf, *Aus dem der Morder Sonderbehandlung' und verwandte Worte in nationalsozialistischen Dokumenten* (Gutersloh, 1963), p. 7.

other "synonyms" have much the same character. So, for example: *Entsprechend behandelt* ("treated appropriately"), *Aussiedlung* ("evacuation"), *Umsiedlung* ("resettlement"), *Auflöckerung* ("thinning out"—as in the removal of inhabitants from a ghetto), *Befriedungsaktion* ("pacification") and *A.B. Aktion,* i.e., *Ausserordentliche Befriedungsaktion* ("special pacification"), *Ausschaltung* ("removal"), *Abwanderung* ("having-been-migrated"), *Saüberung* ("cleansing"), *Sicherheitspolizeilich durchgearbeitet* ("worked through in a Security Police manner")—all were used in place of standard terms for killing or execution. Such usage occurred, moreover, not only in communications issued to the Jewish public when the intention of those issuing the communications was to deceive the Jews in order to minimize the likelihood of resistance, but also in addressing the outside world and, perhaps more significantly, for internal communications as well, among officials who unquestionably knew (who were themselves sometimes responsible for) the linguistic substitutions stipulated by the speech rules. (At times, of course, standard, nonfigurative terms were used for each of these audiences, but the context then was usually an order announcing the execution of individuals who were named, or in warnings directed against specific acts; the orders for larger and more abstract plans of killing under the general aegis of the "Final Solution" were almost always couched in diffuse and abstract terms of the sort noted here.)

The list of such terms, moreover, does not stop with those that refer to killing: the apparatus that would make that act possible also required figurative elaboration. So *Hilfsmittel* ("auxiliary equipment") designated the vans that had been turned into the mobile gas chambers that killed by recycling the carbon monoxide from the vans' engines and which continued to be used elsewhere even after the *Badeanstalten* ("bath arrangements"—i.e., gas chambers) had been constructed at Auschwitz. *Briefaktion* ("letter-action")would refer to coercing new arrivals in the camps to write to relatives or friends in the ghettoes or cities, reassuring them about the prospects of "resettlement." *Gleichschaltung* ("putting into the same gear") could range in meaning from the abolition of divergent political parties to the removal of individuals (although not usually their execution)—in effect the "evening out" of obstacles or impediments.

Such terms, moreover, were not left to the moment or to individual inventiveness; they were part of an official, although evolving, code or set of rules *(Sprachberegelungen)* that identified the words which should not be used and the terms intended to replace them. An explicit example of how these rules were laid down appears in a directive by which the use of "Sonderbehandlung" was announced. This order (dated 26 September 1939) reiterates "the stipulation of the rules in accordance with which the so-called delights of war are to be renamed," and then goes on to designate the abbreviation "Sb" for *Sonderbehandlung* (itself substituted for "killing").

To be sure, even the most resourcefully planned "speech rules" would not anticipate all contingencies, and the requirements of a vocabulary consistent with the act of genocide might well run out of terms insofar as it depended on language that had not yet conceived of the act. The extraordinary phenomenon of the Nazi genocide discloses itself then also in the fact that for some of its features, there simply would be—perhaps *could* be—no satisfactory terms, whether in the language available or by later contrivance, literal or figurative. In order to arrive at such terms, the events themselves would first have to be conceived—and there were at the time features of the genocide (some remain even now, decades later) which evidently posed difficulties even for the imagination. An important example of such difficulty is represented in the term "genocide" itself, which was coined by Rafael Lemkin in the early 1940s in his effort to give a name as well as a definition to the phenomenon exemplified in the Final Solution. The term *genocide,* to be sure, is in the context not a neutral one and would probably not have been assimilated into the Nazi vocabulary by the Nazis themselves (at least as applied to their war against the Jews). But other examples that are not "tendentious" in this way indicate the difficulty *in principle* of finding words for features of the Nazi genocide.

Especially noticeable among these examples are the terms designating the status of the Jews who had been brought to the death camps. The problem of giving a name to the Jews in this role exactly mirrors the extraordinary nature of that role itself. Again: the Jews collectively had been condemned to death by the order to implement the "Final Solution." (No single and explicit written order to this effect has been found, a fact which has led to arguments about whether such an order was ever given, or if it was, whether Hitler issued it, or more bizarrely still, whether Hitler was himself aware that the Final Solution was being implemented. Yet there can be no doubt that such an order *was* given, and with Hitler's authority behind it.)* On the other hand, for "practical" reasons, it was evident that any such order or series of orders could not be carried out instantly but required organization and time; this, together with such other "practical" reasons as the need for skilled labor that the Jews might provide, sometimes argued for delaying the implementation of the order. Thus, distinctions were made on occasion even within the death camps and more often in the concentration camps among those to be killed immediately and those whose execution would be delayed. When the genocidal sentence of death is combined with such gradations of treatment (however temporary), the problem of finding a specific name for the still-living "victims" of such an act is evident. They were to be treated arbitrarily as a matter of principle, with death as the end, but not necessarily immediately; while they lived, they had no rights, not even the right to a specific "death sentence," although they might indeed receive such a sentence if they took some action that was not merely submissive. (*Kadavergehorsam*—"cadaver-obedient"—was the ghoulish term, familiar from its use in the German army and not a code word at all, that designated *this* requirement.) The Jews held in the camps in effect lacked the rights that even animals were assured in the Third Reich. What then could they be called? They were, obviously, "prisoners"—but that term would not distinguish between them and people held and *maintained* in custody for a specified length of time and possibly, then, to be released. For some of the same reasons, they would not be "inmates"—a term which adds the sense of protective custody to the possibility that rehabilitative measures might be part of the design. In the spring of 1945, when the camps still in existence (for example, Buchenwald and Bergen-Belsen) were overrun by the Allied armies, newspapers in the United States (e.g., *The New York Times,* 18 and 19 April 1945) typically spoke about the "slaves" who were found there—the dead as well as the living. This locution was based on the erroneous assumption—which in almost any other circum-

---

* For an assessment of these claims, see Gerald Fleming, *Hitler and the Final Solution* (Berkeley, Calif., 1984); and Eberhard Jäckel, *Hitler in History* (Hanover, N.H., 1984), chap. 3.

stance would have been reasonable—that the main function of the camps was to provide slave labor. But this, too, of course, skews the description, since although Jews in the camps were sometimes used as slave labor and although, like slaves in extreme settings, they lacked legal rights of protection or care, the *main* purpose for which they were in the camps was not to work but to die.

"Victims" is sometimes used in reference to the Jews inside the camps (as well as to those killed outside them)—but again, although obviously accurate in one sense, the conventional association of the term with people killed in individual acts of violence or even in accidents or natural catastrophes does not touch the rationale behind the death camps. (Even the reference to individual "victims" of premeditated murder misses the essential features of deliberation and organization that characterize genocide.) Nor could they be termed "captives," which might suggest both that they had been caught after having been free and that the future awaiting them was contingent. Yet, although in the strict sense they were "condemned" to death, they were not exactly awaiting execution either, since this, again, suggests a definiteness about their status and the fate awaiting them that did not obtain except in the most general sense: starvation, disease, and overwork were officially expected to kill many of the Jews in the camps—but that is not what is meant ordinarily, in judicial terms, by a death sentence. The term *Häftling* that the Nazis themselves usually applied comes close to the sense of "captive" or "prisoner" and is thus also something of a euphemism. (To the extent that *Häftling* implies captivity as part of a specific sentence or as awaiting sentence, it would be simply misleading; to *be* a Jew, as the Nazis had defined that, was itself to have sentence pronounced.) The Nazis had a variety of reasons, symbolic and psychological as well as practical, for tattooing numbers on the people in the camps, but one consequence of the practice was that the number itself would sometimes serve as a means of direct address or reference. The people in the camps devised for themselves the term *KZ-etnik* from the letters of the "Konzentration Lager," a neologism that suggested something novel in their situation, but was not descriptive. (For those who died, the Nazis sometimes explicitly prohibited calling them "victims" or even "corpses," stipulating the term *Figuren* ("figures," "pieces," as in chess). There seems in fact to be *no* term that meets the specific conditions imposed by the act of genocide on those who were subjected to the act, as the Nazis conceived it. Not surprisingly, this same lack seems to recur in respect to the verb(s) associated with the act: "killing," "execution," even "murder"—all miss the distinctive character of the act, although each, to be sure, is within limits accurate. Thus genocide as it evidently stretched the imagination in its own conception, forcing revision in the history of evildoing, also reaches the limits of language as it requires terms to describe *what* it intended and attempted.

It is evident, moreover, that the consequences of genocide for language were not confined to official documents or statements, nor even to explicit decisions about speech rules, although these, too, reached the public domain. So, for example, Goebbels (13 December, 1937) would stipulate that "from today the word 'Volkerbund' ('League of Nations') will no longer be used in the Germans press. This word no longer exists." There was also, as might have been expected, an in some ways still more revealing linguistic "unconscious," the consequences of which appeared in standard usage even when the discussion did not refer to the Final Solution or to military or political matters at all. The inversion of language that results in the figure of the lie may not be as graphic in these more commonplace appearances as it is in terms like *Endlösung,* but the pattern of a general style disclosed by them is in certain ways no less significant. For here it is the image of a general social and cultural order that we see, not only the conscious dictates of a political or military will. And here, too, there is evidence of the same general purpose at once to rationalize language and to subordinate it to authority, that is, to make it into a political instrument which in its own structure would incorporate the features of moral violation that otherwise constitute the lie.

The usage thus introduced reflects in language a genocidal society in its "everyday" life; the linguistic features that might be cited in this connection extend from some that apply to other aspects of culture as well as to language to others that are specific to linguistic usage. The features of repetition and exaggeration or monumentality have often been cited as characteristic of totalitarian "style"—and these were indeed persistent features of Nazi rhetoric (thus, Kenneth Burke's association of Hitler's hold on his audience with the "power of endless repetition")* as they were elsewhere also, for example, in Nazi architecture and drama, particularly in the giant Nazi rallies. Those same features, moreover, extended beyond the official language to common linguistic usage, in journalism and popular fiction as well as in school textbooks. In the latter, too, the style of domination controls the expressive means; language appears as a technological instrument that may serve purposes quite apart from, even in conflict with, the direct representation of events or objects.

The more specific means employed for this purpose cover a spectrum of changes that extend beyond the "style" of figurative discourse to semantic and syntactic alterations as well. Thus, for example, hyperbole is normalized with the common use of exaggerated terms like *einmalig* ("unique"), *historisch* ("historic"), *total* ("total"). *Fanatisch* ("fanatic"), which had the connotation of madness, would now in the Nazi vocabulary count as commendable (and expected, i.e., normal) dedication. The same pattern of repetition and hyperbole was further joined to a conscious effort at defamiliarization: archaic or "folk" words were revived, (e.g., *Mädel* for *Mädchen* ["girl"], *Sippe* for *Familie* ["family"]), and certain foreign words were adapted (e.g., *Aktion* for *Unternehmung*). It may seem that the two latter impulses conflict—one attempting to reach back to German history, the other reaching outside it, to alien sources; but in context, these two are quite consistent. The former is impelled by a mystique of the German past that served as an important ideological element in Nazi doctrine; the latter provides an aura of technological rationality and irrefutability that the Nazis wished now to extend to language as well. Thus, on the one hand, the sources offer the lure of the unfamiliar and so of novelty and power; on the other hand, they conspire to turn a history of ethnic origin into a promise of national destiny (and once again, of power). Again, more generally we infer from this usage the intention to subordinate language itself to political authority,

---

* Kenneth Burke, "The Rhetoric of Hitler's *Battle*," in *The Philosophy of Literacy Form* (Berkeley: University of California Press, 1973), 217–218. See also Harold D. Lasswell, Nathan Leites and Association, *Language of Politics* (New York: G. W. Stewart, 1949), Introduction; and Saul Friedländer, *Reflections of Nazism,* trans. by T. Weyer (New York: Harper & Row, 1984), 50–53.

if only in order to demonstrate that also this common medium of exchange, which often appears in the guise of nature itself, will not escape political domination. The Nazis would not only contrive a language *of* domination, but they intended to demonstrate that language itself was subject to political authority.

The means by which the theme of domination is given a linguistic form are designed in such a way as to leave an audience no option except submission to the spoken or written words that address him. The use of puns and alliteration in Nazi political slogans, for example, forcibly joins words and phrases that have little to do with each other except for the process of assertion itself. Thus: "Die Liebe der SS das Leben der Fürer umgürtet." ("The love of the SS protects the life of the Führer"); or "Das Leben des Führer bleibt nicht ein Wirklichkeit sondern wird zu einer Wahrheit" ("The life of the Führer does not remain a reality but becomes a truth"). An analogous example is the use of conjunctive phrases in contexts the purpose of which is to assert the conjunction rather than to identify related meanings—in such redundant transitions, for instance, as "und damit" and "und mit diesem" ("and thereby" and "and therewith"). It is not only the *act* of conjunction that is intended in such usage, moreover, but the whole that is then constituted (*organisch,* organic, is itself a favorite term): the reader or listener was to see *himself* as part of the whole. Thus, as the conjunctions lead to larger and larger units, the alternatives left to the audience turn out to be those either of full acceptance or of an equally complete denial—the latter, from the point of view of language tantamount to an acceptance of silence and nonexistence. There are no gaps left in the discourse that might be claimed by the listener or reader for questions or objections, or for his proposal of an alternative; the writer or speaker anticipates all the questions that arise or, more characteristically, denies their possibility: the implied audience is to be of one mind with the author.

The implication that things or events are not determinate or accessible unless they are brought together in a discursive whole is also emphasized by the practice of adding suffixes to nouns that attach a *state* of being to references which otherwise might be specific and active: so, for example, *Volkheit* ("peopleness") or *Wehrheit* ("defenseness"). These suffixes identify the thing named as itself indeterminate or tentative—and thus as

174

requiring for "real" existence a state or condition shared with other would-be individuals and provided by a more general and abstract source of being. Thus, what superficially might seem to be a single and independent noun, standing for an individual referent or thing, turns out, more basically, to be part of a larger—by implication, of a single—whole. It requires no great imaginative leap to see in that whole the totalitarian will or its political embodiment in the state.

Again, the features thus identified recurred in popular and informal writing as well as in official documents. (To be sure, given the increasing control of censorship, virtually anything published in Germany—textbooks, newspapers, etc.—after the first years of the Nazi regime would have to be considered an official document.) Admittedly, sustained analysis of stylistic change at this level would require the study of personal correspondence and other informal writing that was not intended to be published, as well as of fiction or poetry that (for literary, not political reasons) moved as far as any publications officially sanctioned could from "normative" usage. The study of these sources is not undertaken here, but, viewed superficially, the stylistic representations of the Nazi vocabulary seem also to recur in these unofficial sources—in academic and literary prose and in personal and casual communications that were not intended for public inspection at all, in what might be called the "private" style. This correlation is predictable if not inevitable: the distinctions that language makes or avoids would be likely to reflect the more general social context in which the distinctions had themselves arisen.

To be sure, like other figures of speech, the literary figure of the lie is accessible to analysis and even before that to the self-consciousness that enables a reader or listener to place it historically in a context of motives, intentions, and consequences. There is also the sense in which all expression, however figurative, is nonetheless literal and truthful; willingly or not, it discloses its own means, art not quite concealing all of art. The "style" of common linguistic usage under the Nazis is subject to this disclosure no less than are the language rules officially commanded: one thing that the will to domination cannot control is the appearance of the will to dominate as seen from the outside—if only an "outside" remains. Viewed from that perspective, the language of genocide, even in its many and complex facets, reveals the intention to turn language itself into an instrument of domination and deceit, enabling in practice and principle an act that controverts the most basic ideals of moral life by the denial of the social reality of language and the reality of human relations beyond that. This is, as has been suggested earlier in these pages, exactly what the physical fact of genocide itself intends and accomplishes: the willing of evil for its own sake quite apart from the consideration of practical consequences. Language itself, we now see, may become a part of that intention, one of its agents—no less revealing of the mind that conceives of and intends genocide than were those other, more obvious instruments of which the will for genocide was to make use.

The assertion made here of a relation between genocide and language does not claim that violence done to language, even on the scale of violence realized by the Nazis, leads inevitably to genocide. Nor does it claim that genocide would only be possible in a setting for which the inversion of values had been so complete as to include language—the currency of thought—as a whole. An alteration in language of the sort described is thus neither necessary nor sufficient as a cause—but again, there is nothing unusual in this limitation either for tracing historical causality in general or for attempting to identify the sources of the Nazi genocide in particular; indeed such limitations would be more likely than elsewhere for an aspect of culture as subtle and diffuse as language. It might be argued that the way we become aware of the role of language as a feature of genocide at all is through being confronted *before* that with the physical act of genocide—although as soon as we hear this, we recognize that even this first awareness may include reference to the violation of language. It is the mind, together with bodies, that genocide acts to destroy; and as language is an essential element of mind, it would be extraordinary if an attack on the latter did not also threaten the former, if the genocidal destruction of a people, directed against every level of its existence, could be envisioned without an accompanying assault on what is thought and said. Like other types of action, evildoing requires a means—and the more elaborate and profound the action, so too the means required for it. The fact that it was the German language that most immediately suffered this violence is an irony of the Nazi genocide, although one that bears on another more general and more familiar irony—that evil-doing claims among its victims the evildoer as well as those whom he had intended to harm.

Then, too, I have not been claiming that the role which language assumes in the Nazi genocide is uniquely located either there or in the phenomenon of genocide as such. The forces contributing to the deformation of language did not begin or end with the Nazi genocide, although there is a connection, causal as well as conceptual, between the two. Both the conception and practice of language that emerged to such coercive effect in the Nazi genocide seem, moreover, to have taken on a strange life of their own subsequently. Evidence of that development is as close at hand as almost any newspaper quotation of political rhetoric in the years since World War II: so the view of language as a technological and impersonal instrument, a view which at the level of political reality was not long ago a radical innovation, now becomes naturalized and familiar, something virtually assumed as native to political language and discourse, even for institutions professedly opposed to and in other basic respects removed in intent from that of the Nazis.

It hardly needs to be said that compared to other aspects of the moral enormity constituted by the Nazi genocide, the inversion of language described here, in the elevation of the lie to a principle of discourse, does not constitute the most immediate or the greatest harm that was done. But since it does not appear by itself but as part of an effort at total destruction, there can be little comfort in this. As people live by representations in the present and by memory in the past, moreover, the role of language in the genocide remains a cogent representation of that event more generally. We find it, in this role, replete with evidence of the will to do evil, the power of the imagination to enlarge on that will, and the capacity for violence which such impulses nourish, inside language or out. These effects can be understood in the character of genocide itself and the requirements imposed by it on those who conceive and "do" it. If it is true that genocide implies the deliberate choice of evil as an end, assuming in the act of killing a conceptualization of the group and the choice of the group as its object, the violation of language in the act of genocide represents something more than only an analogy between language and genocide. It is not only, then, that language becomes morally culpable by its figurative device of the "lie"—but that elements of the lie are also themselves

177

effective causes in the deliberate act of genocide: there is in these both the denial of truth and history—a denial, we learn by way of the Nazi language rules, of which the Nazis themselves were aware. Furthermore, the "objects" of genocide—people and language—which are denied the right to exist are closely related to each other in their group or social character. It is not only individual parts or uses of language that are violated, but language as such, a corporate entity much like the corporate object, the "genos," of genocide itself.

This is not meant to suggest that all evildoing turns out to be one, that any single act entails all others and also the guilt for those others—or more specifically, that genocide and the violation of language are intrinsically related. But it does mean that as evildoing involves always human agents and almost always human victims, there will undoubtedly be more at issue in any single act than what the act itself explicitly designates. Especially in language do we recognize the figure and the moral spirit of its source; there is little to distinguish the linguistic representation from what it is a representation of or from the agent who intends it as a representation. Thus also, the language of genocide, long after the conditions that initially produced it, may persist still, as a challenge to the present as well as to the past. It would be a mistake to imagine that the history of the language of genocide, any more than other consequences of the genocide, ended with the conclusion of the physical act.

The relation between character—whether in the individual or in the group—and language becomes further evident in what started here as analogy but has disclosed itself as more than that: in the common feature of domination that in the name of principle engendered both the act of genocide and the instrumental role ascribed to language. On both sides of that analogy, distinctions based on evidence and moral principle are overridden; categories and distinctions devised and willed by the agent are made to seem natural and necessary, and this is itself part of the intention. Not only language but logic are brought inside history by these efforts, moreover; and not only are the cultural appearances of these domains brought into history, but so also are the "objects" they ostensively refer to. There is nothing in language, as in humanity more generally, that is exempt from the controlling intention. The will to do evil through the medium of genocide is in fact the will to transcend *all* limits or restrictions, and this intention which includes language among its objects, produces a lie of even a larger order than does the use of language specifically tied to the act of genocide itself. In this increasingly generalized consequence, the moral lie comes close to being absolute, denying the figurative representation of truth in all its forms and even the possibility of truth itself; the moral lie chooses evil as its good on grounds of principle, and this means that no subordinate purpose is acknowledged or chosen by the agent of genocide which is not evil. For the *language* of genocide, the change is smaller but hardly less noticeable. In it, the lie becomes a figure of speech, when it had been the native purpose of figurative language, arguably of *all* language, to disclose and to enlarge, not to conceal or to diminish, much less to destroy, still less to destroy completely.

Index